Researching Online

Second Edition

D0140088

David Munger

Daniel Anderson
University of North Carolina

Bret Benjamin
University of Texas—Austin

Christopher Busiel
University of Texas—Austin

Bill Parades-Holt
University of Texas—Austin

LONGMAN

An imprint of Addison Wesley Longman, Inc.

*New York • Reading, Massachusetts • Menlo Park, California • Harlow, England
Don Mills, Ontario • Sydney • Mexico City • Madrid • Amsterdam*

ditor-in-Chief: Patricia A. Rossi
Publishing Partner: Anne Smith
Senior Editor: Lisa Moore
Supplements Editor: Donna Campion
Text Design: DTC
Electronic Page Makeup: DTC

Researching Online, 2/e
by David Munger, et al.

ISBN: 0-321-05117-3 (spiral-bound)
         0-321-02714-0 (perfect-bound)

1 2 3 4 5 6 7 8 9 10 - CRW - 01 00 99 98

Contents

Preface

Books still have some advantages over online materials. Most people can't carry a Web page with them to class.* Most people have monitors that are too small to display the text of a book like this concurrently with a project they're working on. Many people are still more comfortable with the authority of books. Books are substantially easier on the eyes than computer monitors. To borrow a computer term, because books feature a higher resolution display, they can convey more information on a page than computers. To borrow another, books utilize a remarkably simple interface, carefully honed through years of tradition.

When you think about it that way, *Researching Online, Second Edition,* might be the best way to learn about research on the Internet. Of course, if you prefer electronic texts, the complete text of this book is also available at *http://longman.awl.com/kennedy/*.

Researching Online shows students how to do research on the Internet in an easy-to-follow, step-by-step format. It's written in plain English, with clear examples of the type of materials students may encounter in their own research. The Internet is presented in the order that students will most likely encounter it: first, they learn how to get on-line. Then they learn about Internet resources like e-mail, the Web, and newsgroups. Finally, they get clear, easy to follow instructions on creating their own Web pages. This edition features a new chapter on researching literature on the Internet, with dozens of links to help students get started.

---

* Only *most* because at Carnegie Mellon University, students can! Fully half of the campus is connected to a wireless network with Internet access via laptop computers.

Everything about *Researching Online* has been designed to make it the most useful possible tool for anyone doing research on the Internet. Its compact size allows it to and consume little desk space in crowded computer labs. Specialized vocabulary is **bold and underlined** to alert readers to terms defined in the glossary. Text users must input is displayed in a `special typeface` to make easy to recognize. URLs are displayed in ***bold italic*** and without confusing angle brackets. Most importantly, critical concepts are both explained in the text and reinforced visually with real-world examples.

Features in this edition

Completely reorganized to place the Web first

Now that the Web is the most significant component of the Internet, *Researching Online* reflects that fact by giving the Web a more prominent placement in the book. Other Internet resources, such as Telnet, Gopher, FTP, IRCs, MOOs, MUDs, and to a lesser extent, Usenet newsgroups and listservs, are becoming increasingly marginalized, and their placement in the book now reflects that trend.

World Wide Web examples

The chapter on the World Wide Web includes many real-world examples, including several different types of Web searches.

Coverage of advanced Web searching techniques

Researching Online offers unparalleled coverage of advanced techniques like the "link" command, multiple search engines, and specialized search engines. In addition, coverage of advanced browsing techniques shows students how to take advantage of the power contained in their own Web browsers.

Easy to understand chapter on building Web sites

The Web site chapter is structured with a process-oriented approach. Instead of just listing HTML commands, it shows how to build a Web site the way real designers do it, with substantial coverage of six key phases in Web site design. HTML coding is presented as just one step in this process. Students learn HTML coding by watching a site being developed, from basic text content to complete HTML tags.

Continuous research paper themes throughout the text

The examples in *Researching Online* follow three topics throughout the book ("Is Microsoft a monopoly?" "Are black filmmakers disfavored at the Oscars?" "Is free verse poetry?"). As students read the book, they become more engaged because all the examples come from these realistic research topics.

E-mail chapter

The e-mail chapter provides clear guidance on the use of e-mail conventions like "smileys," abbreviations, and "ASCII art." It also provides extensive coverage of listservs, giving them a section of their own.

New literature research chapter

A new chapter on literature research, including links to literature Web sites and other Internet resources, makes *Researching Online* a more valuable resource for English students and teachers.

Section on using online vs. traditional sources

Researching Online gives students useful guidance on the issue of using online versus traditional sources. Many students have been confused by this issue, and now they have a place to turn to determine where the most useful research information will appear.

Guidance on determining the reliability of online sources

The book contains specific guidance on how to assess the reliability and validity of an electronic information source—which is imperative in any kind of research. The section includes links to Internet resources which expand on this coverage.

Acknowledgments

This book evolved out of the groundbreaking book *Teaching Online* by Daniel Anderson, Bret Benjamin, Christopher Busiel, and Bill Paredes-Holt. The three chapters on older but still very valuable Internet resources from that book have been retained almost intact. Christopher Busiel and Tom Maeglin deserve special recognition because they wrote the first edition of *Researching Online*. Karen Milholland provided most of the research behind the literature research chapter, as well as a sounding board for ideas and much needed assistance at crunch time. Robert Cline,

Greta Munger, and Jim Park gave tremendous insight into the power of the Internet. Jimmy and Nora Munger demonstrated how easy computers can be to use and learn from. Anne Smith, Lisa Moore, and Patricia Rossi at Longman were rock-solid in their support of this book. Jennifer Ahrend provided brilliant copyediting. Donna Campion helped immeasurably in seeing it through to the finish. Thanks again to all who contributed.

Chapter 1

Introduction

It's 3:00 A.M., your paper is due in six hours, you need one more source to complete your argument, and every library in your time zone is closed.

or

You're not sure about the reliability of a source you want to use in a paper, but it's too new to have published reviews.

or

You need to find every reference to *eyes* in *Macbeth.*

or

You'd like to collaborate on a biology project with your lab partner from last semester—but she's in Germany this term on a semester abroad.

The **Internet** can be part of the solution to each of these problems. For finding that one last source at 3:00 A.M., try a search engine on the **World Wide Web**. To verify the reliability of a source for which you can't find a published review, try posting a query on a **Usenet newsgroup**. To search for specific words or phrases in Shakespeare's plays, try the The Complete Plays of William Shakespeare, at ***http://www.ke .com.au/cgi-bin/texhtml?form=Shake.*** To collaborate with someone in another part of the world, communicate with **e-mail**, then work interactively using an **IRC** or a **MUD**.

Can the Internet answer all of your research questions? Well, it doesn't contain the entire archives of the Library of Congress or even every back issue of the *New York Times* (not yet, anyway). It can't perform original research experiments or help you communicate with someone who doesn't have Internet access. And while it can help you reach people and

1

resources on the other side of the world, it's certainly no substitute for live, one-on-one interaction with real people and real things.

The Internet is at its best when it helps make your research experience easier, more thorough, and more collaborative. At other times, it can be frustrating, biased, and inaccurate. This book will help guide you through the process of integrating online sources into your research.

How the Internet can inform your research

The Internet can be thought of as an enormous, constantly evolving conversation in which users meet to discuss almost any imaginable topic. There are dozens of ways you can benefit from using the Internet; for instance, you can easily:

- Access important information to support your research.
- Communicate with authors of important sources or experts in various fields of study.
- Meet online with other researchers to discuss a common topic.
- Design and "publish" an interactive, multimedia site on the World Wide Web, offering a research paper, links to other Internet resources about the topic, video clips of major figures, and forums for conversation among users.

The Internet is a worldwide network of computers which are connected to each other in many different ways. Each of these different sorts of connections, called **protocols**, is useful for different kinds of work. The most important Internet services, and the protocols they follow, are listed below.

World Wide Web. Now the most important part of the Internet, the Web allows you to quickly navigate through millions of **hypertext** sites containing images, text, sound, and motion pictures using browsers that are easy and intuitive to use. The Web uses the HyperText Transfer Protocol (HTTP).

E-mail. E-mail allows you to quickly exchange messages and computer files with anyone connected to the Internet. E-mail uses the Simple Mail Transfer Protocol (SMTP).

Usenet newsgroups. Newsgroups are a vast collection of specialized electronic bulletin boards where (usually) anyone can post or respond to a message. Usenet uses the News Protocol.

Listservs. A specialized type of e-mail, listservs are moderated or unmoderated discussion groups on specified topics.

Telnet, FTP, and Gopher. Older parts of the Internet, these are ways of accessing files and programs on distant computers.

IRCs and MU*s. These are services which allow you to communicate with other users in real time, following one of several possible protocols.

Limitations of online research

You should be aware of some of the problems presented by the Internet, so that you can overcome them in your research. Among the problems you should be aware of when using the Internet are the following:

- The temptation to play online and the risk of losing sight of your purpose.
- The vast volume of information on the Internet and the difficulties of managing it.
- The steep learning curve and prohibitive expense of some applications and Internet technologies.
- The fact that, despite its global scale, the Internet (and indeed personal computers in general) is still heavily marked by class, race, gender, and geography.

Always try to determine whether the extra work or expense of certain Internet media merits their use on a particular project. If you master a few basic operations of Internet applications, learn a few strategies for finding and evaluating sources, and keep focused while online, chances are the Internet will reward you for your efforts.

It is important to remember that the Internet is *biased.* The Internet was developed as a means of collaboration for people working on computers—initially scientists in the U.S. defense industry. As it was developed, people began to see how easy it would be add more and more computers to the network. If a computer network already exists, it is a relatively simple matter to connect that network to the Internet—thus creating a network that connects many, if not most, of the world's computer networks. Bias is introduced because while it is a (relatively) simple matter to connect computer networks, other media are not so cooperative. Film, books, television, oral traditions, newspapers, radio—

these are more difficult to add to a network of computers. Information contained in these media is less well represented on the Internet than that of computerized media—databases, text files, digitized images and sounds, and so on.

While many media are *becoming* computerized—especially printed media—this computerization is not uniform. It's most prevalent in developed ("First World") countries—largely because they can afford it. So there is a bias in the Internet toward the industrialized world, which is in turn biased toward Western men.

There is also an issue of *copyright*. Because information on the Internet is so easy to copy, the Internet is biased toward non-copyrighted material. So it's easier to find the complete works of Shakespeare on the Internet than it is to find the complete works of Stephen King.

When to use online sources; When to use traditional sources

Whenever you begin a research project, once you've decided on a topic it's always best to formulate a research plan or proposal. Depending on your plan, sometimes traditional sources will provide you with the most options and sometimes online sources will. Here are a few concerns to keep in mind when trying to determine whether to use online sources or traditional ones:

1. **Timeliness.** In many cases, particularly with newsgroups and listservs, the Internet can provide more up-to-date information than traditional sources. And while daily newspapers offer a reliable, traditional research source, most major newspapers are now available on the World Wide Web, with searchable indexes of past issues.
2. **Type of resources you need.** Depending on your project's requirements, the type of resources you need may be more readily available online, or they may be more likely to be found in a traditional library. For example, your instructor may require that all (or a certain number) of your research sources be from academic books or refereed journal articles. In this case, though you may want to use an online service to locate resources, you will most likely find the actual resources in a library. On the other hand, if your instructor requires that you interview an expert in a

field, you may be more likely to make that contact via
the Internet.

3. **Accessibility**. If everyone had access to a library with
thousands of journal subscriptions and millions of vol-
umes, traditional sources might often be the best option. However, most of us don't have that luxury, so
online sources become a more important component
of the research process.

4. **Reliability**. Pay close attention to the matters discussed in the following section, "How to evaluate an
electronic source." You need to weigh the issues discussed above with issues of reliability discussed below
in order to determine which resource is more useful
for your topic.

How to evaluate an electronic source

One of the most important virtues of the Internet is its
universality. For about a hundred dollars, anyone can regis-
ter a World Wide Web address and have as much of a Web
presence as Microsoft or IBM. The Internet has no gate-
keeper (for that matter, it has no single, central gate).

While the universality of the Internet can be good in
that it allows previously marginalized voices to be heard, it
also adds a new layer of difficulty for researchers. The gatekeepers of traditional research sources—editors, academics, and librarians—have always made it a relative cer-
tainty that any source in a college library meets a basic
standard of reliability and relevance. Since the Internet
lacks those gatekeepers, you're just as likely to encounter
uninformed drivel there as you are to find an example of
true brilliance.

Additionally, materials found online will often differ a
great deal from those in print. Resources may feature graphics, sound, and video, for example. What's more, Internet
sources may have a more (or less) impressive appearance
than traditional "published" articles.

When you're evaluating an electronic source, above all,
you must *read critically*. Ask questions, and never assume the
source is an authority. Here are some guidelines you can use
to evaluate an electronic source:

- Who is the author?
- Is a link to the author's **home page** (see page 70)
  and/or e-mail contact information provided?

- Does the author have an academic or professional affiliation?
- Who is the sponsor of the resource? An academic organization? A business?
- What are the potential biases/hidden agendas of the author and/or the sponsor of the resource?
- Is the resource regularly updated? Are the links provided up to date?
- Does the resource follow good principles of design and proper grammar and style? (*Note:* good design is not necessarily "flashy." A simple, conservative site can be more tasteful than one bristling with graphics and sound effects.)
- Are the articles reviewed by peers? (*Note:* Beware of "Top 500 Web site" awards and the like—always check *them* out using the standards given here. There are even Web sites which are completely devoted to giving out phony awards—for a hilarious example, check out ***http://www.thecorporation.com/icon/icon.html*.)

Writing instructors and librarians have recognized the difficulty in evaluating electronic sources, and some have attempted to generate uniform criteria for evaluating these sources. You may want to check out the Using Cybersources Web site at ***http://www.devry-phx.edu/lrnresrc/dowsc/integrty.htm*** for a detailed set of guidelines on how to evaluate a Web source, as well as links to other sites with more suggestions.

How the Internet works

Client/Server interaction

One way of organizing the Internet is in terms of **clients** and **servers**. Unfortunately, this vocabulary has often confused users of the Internet, because "client" and "server" already have English-language meanings, and those "standard" definitions are slightly different from the way the terms are used to describe the Internet.

If you are a customer in a real restaurant, you are the client, and your server is the person who brings you your food. If we apply this analogy to the Internet, however, the meanings of those terms change. If the Internet were a restaurant, there would a different *server* for each type of food (soup, solid food, drinks, etc.) and the *clients* would be the containers customers need for each type of food. In addition, customers would be required to provide their own containers. The "food" of the Internet is information. *Clients* are programs which users can use to send or receive a particular type of information, and *servers* are programs that network computers use to send or receive a particular type of information to or from clients.

Servers reside on network-connected machines. What distinguishes a server program from other software is that it provides files and information for use by client programs. These clients are a separate set of programs which "talk" to servers and access the data they offer according to specific **protocols** which act as a sort of "language" between Internet clients and servers.

For example, to send an e-mail message to the president of the United States, you use a client e-mail program (like Eudora or Navigator) on your computer to compose the message. The client sends the message to your college or university's mail server, a program residing on a networked computer. That server sends the message to the server in the White House (possibly with several intermediate steps). Then, the president (or more likely, a White House intern) uses another client program on a computer to check for mail on the White House server, at which point the server sends the message to the president's computer, where he can use his e-mail client software to read your message. You can try this out for yourself. The president's e-mail **address** (see Chapter 2) is *president@whitehouse.gov.*

Other types of clients, such as e-mail programs like Pine and browser programs like Lynx, actually reside on servers, allowing users to read mail and browse the World Wide Web using only a terminal or modem software. For the most part, this book assumes you are accessing the Internet using client software that resides on your own computer (**workstation** client software), which we recommend because it is generally easier to use than server-based client software, allowing you to focus on ideas, rather than technology.

Connecting to the Internet

Connecting via the campus network. Most colleges and universities have a network of computers that is connected to the Internet. In many cases, computers are available for student use in computer labs, the library, or in dorms. All the necessary client software will be installed on the computers; all you need to do is learn to use the client software on those computers, and you're in business (see Chapters 2–6). For e-mail, you'll need to establish an e-mail account—usually handled through your campus computer services department.

Connecting using your own computer. If you have your own computer, getting connected to the Internet is a little more complicated—but once you're connected, it's a lot more convenient than relying on public computers. If you have a brand-new computer, it's very likely that all the client software you need is already installed on your computer. If you have inherited an older computer, especially one that has never been connected to the Internet, you may have to do a bit of scrambling to obtain the client software you need. At the bare minimum, you need a connection program (usually a PPP program and a TCP/IP program), a **mailreader**, and a <u>Web browser</u>. An easy way to get all this software is to upgrade your computer to the newest operating system—either Windows or Mac—which will include Internet connectivity software.

Direct Access. Many institutions offer direct access to the Internet in campus dorms. If you live on campus and your campus offers this service, it's worthwhile to purchase any hardware you need to connect directly—the connection will be much faster and more reliable than any other means of Internet connection. Usually all you'll need is an Ethernet card and a login name and password.

Dial-up Access. If you don't live on campus, or if your dorm isn't wired for direct access, then you must connect via dial-up access. You'll need a modem for your computer and access to a phone line. Contact your computer services department to learn the dial-in phone number and to obtain a login name and password. If your school doesn't have a dial-in number, you can still get Internet access by subscribing to an Internet service provider. These services will often offer a flat monthly rate for unlimited Internet access, usually around $20 per month. Some of the most popular Internet service providers are AT&T, IBM, Mindspring, and America Online.

URLs: Addresses on the Internet

The Internet has no center. There is no single computer or group of computers in the "middle" of the Internet. There isn't even a "map" or physical representation of how all the computers on the Internet are connected. The only thing everyone on the Internet has agreed upon is how resources are named. Every resource on the Internet has a unique name, different from every other resource on the Internet. Once you know a resource's name, you don't need to know where it is, what kind of computer it's on, or how to get there. All the information you need to find every resource on the Internet is included in the name itself.

Names on the Internet are called **URLs** (Uniform Resource Locators). A URL has several parts:

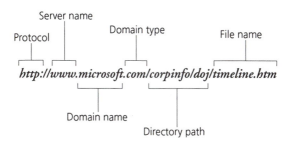

The protocol indicates the type of link to be made with the server. In this case, it's **http:**, which stands for hypertext transfer protocol—the protocol used for all resources on the World Wide Web. The **domain** name is registered by the Web site owner, in this case the Microsoft Corporation. The server name (usually *www* for Web sites) refers to the server the site owner uses to host the Web site. The domain type indicates what type of organization the owner is, here a commercial organization. The **directory path** reflects the overall organization of the Web site. This resource is located in the *doj* subdirectory of the *corpinfo* directory. The **file name** is the name the site owner has given to the particular resource you're looking at, here a timeline of the Department of Justice's investigation of Microsoft for possible antitrust violations. Note that slashes (not backslashes, as in DOS directories) are used to separate directory names from each other and from the domain name and file name. Two slashes are used to separate the protocol from the domain name.

When you say a URL, you can save time by using a few common conventions. If the person you're speaking to knows you're referring to a Web address, you can leave out the *http://*. Then say "www dot microsoft dot com slash corpinfo slash doj slash timeline dot htm." E-mail addresses also include the @ sign, pronounced "at." However, when you refer to URLs in formal research, always give the complete URL.

Chapter 2

Initiating Conversation: E-Mail

What is e-mail?

If the Internet can be described as a continuously evolving conversation, then **electronic mail** (e-mail) is the basic technology that allows you to speak up and be heard. E-mail is a building block of Internet communication and composition. The audience for e-mail messages can encompass a single instructor or student, a group of students, the class as a whole, a campus e-mail **discussion list**, or a world-wide audience made up of personal contacts or subscribers to a **listserv**.

The basic tool for sending and receiving e-mail is called a **mailreader** (also known as a "mail client"). While it may be possible to exchange e-mail without a mailreader, these programs provide an easy interface for reading, composing, posting, and **downloading** e-mail messages. Common mailreaders include Eudora (for Macintosh systems) and Weudora (for Windows and DOS systems). The major World Wide Web **browsers**, Netscape Navigator and Microsoft Internet Explorer, also include mailreaders. It is also easy to find many other mailreaders with different features and characteristics. Many mailreader programs can be downloaded from the Internet as **freeware** (software programs distributed free of charge).

Mailreaders send and receive messages through **mail servers**, programs on computers connected to the Internet which organize, store, and distribute e-mail messages to various users. Servers exchange with each other (often through a chain of several servers in different locations across the country or worldwide) using two-part e-mail **addresses**.

11

Addresses and their elements

A typical e-mail address contains two elements. The **mailbox name** or **user's name** appears before the **@** sign, and the **domain** information, representing the server that provides e-mail to the user, follows the @ sign. A sample message might use these addresses:

```
From: dmunger-dtc@mindspring.com
To: president@whitehouse.gov
```

The mailbox name of the sender is *dmunger-dtc*. The recipient's mailbox name is *president*.

The domain generally contains information about the organization and organization type. Elements of the domain are separated by a period (.) generally called a dot.

Here, the sender's domain includes the name of the organization, "mindspring," and an abbreviation describing the type of organization, "com" (commercial). The mailbox of the recipient, president, is registered with the organization "whitehouse," classified as "gov" (government).

In the United States, the standard domain types are:

```
.edu = educational institution
.com = commercial organization
.gov = government organization
.mil = military institution
.org = non-profit organization
.net = (often) Internet service provider
```

Outside the United States, domain names usually end in a two-letter element indicating the country of origin: for example, .jp (Japan), .nl (the Netherlands), and .eg (Egypt).

Many mailreaders allow you to save addresses in a file called an address book which makes it unnecessary to retype an address. In addition, many provide ways to keep special addresses called nicknames on file. A **nickname** is a list of addresses represented by one name. When a message is sent to the nickname, the computer sends that message to each of the addresses in the nickname file.

Getting connected

We recommend that all students set up an e-mail account. Most colleges and universities have already incorporated computer and Internet fees into tuition costs, so they generally offer "free" or very inexpensive e-mail accounts to students and faculty. Although some students will inevitably have problems along the way, setting up an account is usually a fairly simple process. For more information on Internet connection, see pages 7–8.

Setting up an e-mail account may take a little time, so request your account very early in the semester. Learn about your systems by reading any handouts with detailed step-by-step instructions. Since schools frequently change e-mail procedures from semester to semester as they expand their computer services, bear in mind that some of the instructions may be incorrect. To verify that your account is working, send yourself a test message.

Using mailreaders and servers

Mail servers are programs on Internet-connected machines which store and distribute electronic messages. A user has three basic options for accessing these servers:

1. **Telnet Client.** The most basic, but also the most limited, way to work with e-mail is through a connection to a remote machine's mail server via a <u>Telnet</u> client. It is possible to read and send messages with this connection; however, the **interface** is quite awkward.
2. **Mail-Reading Client.** You will probably prefer to use a mail-reading client when working with e-mail. Making a Telnet connection to a remote machine and activating a mail-reading client provides an easier interface and offers more features than connecting directly to the mail server. For example, the main menu of Pine, a Unix-based mailreader, looks like this:

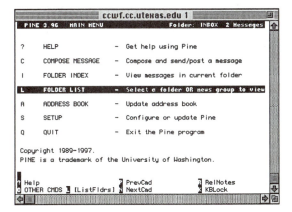

In this format, you can perform a variety of functions with keystrokes. Your mail remains on the server, but saved messages can be sorted into folders. An address book feature lets you quickly access frequently-used addresses.

3. **Workstation mail-reading client.** Workstation mail-reading clients reside on your personal computer and provide the most versatile interface for handling e-mail operations. These programs (Eudora is probably the most popular and is available as freeware) retrieve mail from the mail server and bring it to your machine. Like server-based mailreaders, workstation clients allow you to create nicknames and offer features like the ability to send formatted documents as attachments and to organize incoming mail into directories or mailboxes for later use. But with a workstation client, you also have access to a variety of mouse-driven menu commands and other features. You can read mail and compose messages in multiple, separate windows.

By clicking on items across the top bar, you can set such features as "text-wrap" at the end of lines, automatically save a copy of the message in your "out" mailbox, and control whether or not to use your signature file (which Eudora saves for you in another window). The button which reads "queue" prepares this message for mailing, but the outgoing message will not be sent until the user selects a menu command to send all her queued messages. This feature is

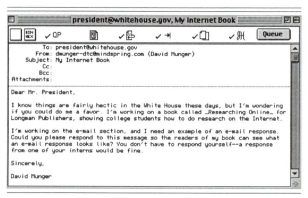

Figure 2.1: An e-mail message composed on a workstation client

useful if you want to minimize the time you are actually connected to the Internet (if a modem and a phone share the same line, for example, or your Internet access is billed by the minute). If the user were to change a particular setting, the "queue" button would instead say "send," and clicking it would deliver the message immediately.

Information about your account is easily saved by workstation mailreaders like Eudora:

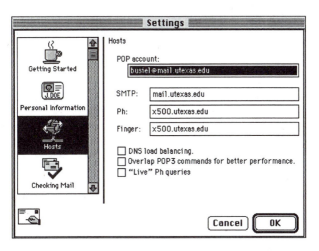

Once you set up the information you will never have to retype your e-mail address, your signature file, or other information. Of course, you will always have access to the configurations, so you can continue modifying the mailreader's functions to your liking.

Classroom uses for e-mail

You can use e-mail in any of the following ways:

- To connect with members of the class on an individual basis and with the instructor outside of class and office hours. E-mail can be especially useful when an unexpected problem or question arises, or when other settings are inappropriate or uncomfortable for asking the question.
- To make inquiries to the instructor, if you have missed class or have a question about an assignment.

- To turn in papers or other homework, to which instructors can respond by e-mailing comments back to you.
- To receive materials particularly relevant to a project, from **listservs** (see page 18), **browsing** sessions (see Chapter 3), other students, or your instructor.

E-mail is also an invaluable tool for collaborating with others:

- You can e-mail peer review partners drafts and comments with the advantage of being able to ask questions and carry on a dialogue.
- When working on collective projects with a small group, you can use e-mail to brainstorm about ideas, share work you have completed individually, or coordinate times to meet as a group.
- You can e-mail resources and materials that you have found with students who have similar research topics.

E-mail etiquette

By its nature, e-mail tends to be less formal than regular mail ("snail mail"). Some have suggested that e-mail compares more closely with spoken conversation than formal letter writing. That's probably a good thing, because it allows people to concentrate on getting their message across quickly instead of focusing on decorum. However, you should still take care when composing a message, because unlike spoken conversation, an e-mail message cannot convey the subtle nuances of speech such as intonation and facial expression.

A debate is currently raging about whether messages should contain unedited typographical errors and abbreviations like *BTW* ("by the way"), *FWIW* ("for what it's worth") or *IMHO* ("in my humble opinion"), *msg* ("message"), *mtg* ("meeting"), or *shd* ("should"). One side of the argument suggests that the immediacy of e-mail is diminished when writers must take time to follow all the rigors of academic writing. Others argue that the development of an Internet "code" of communication unnecessarily excludes people who aren't "in the know" while offering a convenient excuse for those who haven't made the effort to learn to communicate properly. A good rule of thumb: when you don't know the recipient well enough to address them by their first name, use conservative language in your e-mail.

Figure 2.2: An example of an e-mail with a reply quotation

Another e-mail convention arose because of the ease with which computer technology reproduces text. When you **reply** to an e-mail message, you can usually include the original message in the response. The e-mail convention for quoting indicates the text that is quoted from the original message with an **angle bracket** (>) before each line of text. Most mailreaders automatically quote the whole text of the preceding message into their reply, so reply quotations can get quite long with little or no effort of your own.

Each time you quote a message, an additional angle bracket will appear before each line. This nesting of quotations continues until one reader decides that there is no need to include the older text, and deletes it. Because e-mail messages are read with varying frequency by different users, you may want to include the original question or issue for clarity. While an unnecessarily long reply quotation can be an annoyance, it can be useful to "overhear" part of the original conversation or to analyze the original message a second time. To cut down on bulk, you can edit out the less significant portions of the reply quotation to draw attention to the most important material. Make sure you contextualize this material in your response.

What is a listserv?

A **listserv**, also known as a "mailing list" or "list," is a program which allows e-mail to be sent to a group of addresses simultaneously. (Throughout this text we will use the term "listserv" generically to denote a range of mailing list programs including Listserv, Majordomo, and Listproc.) Though listservs vary according to function, type, and administration, each listserv defines a narrow subject area which all posts are expected to fall within. For example, the discussion list *MODBRITS* carefully defines its scope as "Modern British and Irish Literature: 1895–1955," and participants are expected to abide by the list's geographic and chronological limits or provide a good rationale for ranging outside them.

Make sure you use listservs according to conventions of Internet etiquette, or **netiquette**. Don't send a message to a list just to pass the time or to try to sell a car (unless the list is for the purpose of selling used cars). For most lists, posts like this would be frowned upon and might result in a number of angry messages (or **flames**) from list members. Some lists have moderators who screen messages before sending them to the full list in order to ensure their relevance. Repeated inflammatory or "off-topic" messages from a user can result in removal from the list. Remember that your message is going to a large audience. Ask yourself if your message is likely to be useful to all the members of the list. Also remember that your issue may have been discussed before you became a member of the list.

Make sure you follow a listserv discussion for a period of time to clarify the nature of the listserv's audience and learn what constitutes an interesting or convincing message on that list. Sometimes, the boundaries of allowable topics on a list are very narrowly defined. For example, the *h-latam* list (a discussion of Latin American history) specifically defines its subject to exclude current events in Latin America. Because the list sees its function as providing a level-headed discussion of "historical" events, especially as these relate to teaching history, potentially heated political discussions of more recent events in Latin America are discouraged. A post discussing causes and effects of the Zapatista uprising in Chiapas, Mexico, for instance, would not be allowed on the list unless it was directed solely to bibliographic source material or pedagogical concerns.

For gathering substantive research material, the most useful lists are those posting items like news stories, articles, documents, and expert commentary. However, you should not give up on a list simply because it focuses on discussion, for you can learn a lot by keeping track of and participating in active listserv debates. You will see how opinions are formed, revised, and complicated, and how multiple perspectives can inform a topic.

Along with the research possibilities provided by listservs, e-mail can be an effective tool for transferring and gathering other types of information. For instance, many online library catalogs and databases allow users to mail information to their accounts. When you find a useful online articles, for instance, you can collect that information easily by e-mailing yourself the material. Once you receive the material in electronic form, you can refer back to the piece at a later date or cut and paste quotations into your paper (with proper acknowledgment, of course).

Using listservs to initiate research conversations

Your instructor may create class listservs or __nicknames__ to make announcements, revise reading or meeting schedules, forward supplementary material, start discussion, or ask for feedback on a particular topic. Lists and nicknames also give you the opportunity to contribute material for course reading and to share relevant resources with the entire class.

Joining conversations outside of the classroom will illustrate the commitments of writers to their discussion of issues and ideas, and will demonstrate that your writing can be important in a larger context. Using listservs can give you access to the opinions of experts. This access to information is a useful stimulus for creating a topic and finding a way to enter a conversation. For example, depending on the listserv, you might come across an index of sources about a research topic or gather current information on a contemporary debate or event.

Besides drawing on the conversations of subscribers to a list, you can ask questions, post your own opinions and receive reactions to the arguments you are developing for class. Don't expect the list to write your paper for you or answer obvious questions. If you post a message like "Can anyone out there help me with my *Hamlet* paper?" or "What was the name of the guy who wrote *Catcher in the Rye?*" you will likely receive some hostile responses and few, if any, useful replies. But if you are able to engage the audience with either an interesting argument or an important category of research or analysis, you will likely receive many useful citations and suggestions for further thought. Of course, you can easily save all of these messages on a diskette and retrieve them when you need them. You can also forward messages to an instructor, other students, or people outside the classroom.

How to subscribe to a listserv

Finding listservs on your research topic

The easiest way to find a listserv is to do a search on the **World Wide Web** (see Chapter 3 for more information on browsing the Web). Point your browser to a mailing list **search engine** like *http://www.liszt.com/* or *http://tile.net /lists/*. There, you can search using **keywords** appropriate to your topic or browse through lists of mailing lists that may be of interest to you.

If you're not sure about a listserv, just subscribe to it for a few days to see if it's useful. If it's not useful to you, you can easily unsubscribe.

Subscribing to a listserv

Subscribing to a listserv is complicated by the fact that there are three major types of listservs: **Listserv**, **Listproc**, and **Majordomo**. Fortunately, it's easy to distinguish between the three types, because the address you e-mail to subscribe always begins with either *listserv, listproc,* or *major-domo*. Never type anything in the subject line, regardless of the type of list you're subscribing to.

Listserv. To subscribe to this type of list, send e-mail to the administrative address for the list you want to subscribe to. For example if you want to subscribe to the African American Women's Literature list, you send the following e-mail message:

```
To: listserv@cmuvm.csv.cmich.edu
subscribe AAWOMLIT your name
```

Don't literally type "your name," unless that's what it says on your birth certificate. If your name is Fred Jones, type that in place of *your name*. The convention in this book is to indicate where you need to fill in your own information by using *italic* type. By the way, one of the most common mistakes beginning computer users make is to literally type in everything they see in the documentation. Whenever you're learning a new program, take a moment to see if the documentation has a special way of indicating information you need to provide yourself—usually, you'll find the going much easier.

Listproc. Subscribing to a listproc works the same way as a listserv. For example, to subscribe to the listproc American Literature, send the following e-mail:

```
To: listproc@lists.missouri.edu
subscribe AMLIT-L your name
```

Majordomo. Since Majordomo servers aren't as sophisticated as Listserv or Listproc, you usually need to include your e-mail address in the subscribe message. For example, to subscribe to the Postcolonial list, send the following e-mail:

```
To: majordomo@jefferson.village.virginia.edu
subscribe postcolonial your e-mail address
```

Unsubscribing to a listserv

To unsubscribe from the lists above, send the following messages:

Listserv

```
To: listserv@cmuvm.csv.cmich.edu
signoff AAWOMLIT
```

Listproc

```
To: listproc@lists.missouri.edu
signoff AMLIT-L
```

Majordomo

```
To: majordomo@jefferson.village.virginia.edu
unsubscribe postcolonial your e-mail address
```

Emoticons and other e-mail miscellany

Many Internet users attempt to express sarcasm and light-hearted emotion by using **emoticons** (usually called

:-)	basic smiley
;-)	winking happy smiley
;-(	crying smiley
:-{	mustache
:-}X	bow-tie-wearing smiley
@:-}	smiley just back from the hairdresser
C=:-)	chef smiley
8(:-)	Mickey Mouse
:———}	you lie like pinnochio
[:-)	smiley wearing a walkman
X:-)	little kid with a propeller beanie

Table 2.1: A small sampling of smileys
Taken from *ftp://ftp.wwa.com/pub/Scarecrow/Misc/Smilies*

smileys). Smileys are roughly the Internet equivalent of a wink, and about as sophisticated. Though they often denote a lack of careful writing, smileys sometimes help clarify the author's intention. The basic smiley is a sideways happy face :-) (tilt your head to the left to read it) although a host of others can be used to express a broad range of emotions. Though a writer might incorporate a smiley in informal prose, it would be preferable in a formal composition to use words to convey irony effectively. Remember, if you say something truly offensive, adding a smiley after it isn't going to do a lot to cool down the offended party.

Another way of personalizing e-mail communication is by adding a **signature** or **sig file** to a message. A signature is a section of text automatically appended to the bottom of e-mail messages. Signatures serve as a way to identify the author and place her socially, professionally, and personally. Besides supplying the writer's e-mail address to facilitate replies, a signature will often carry a writer's professional or academic affiliations, an indication of whether the current message is personal or professional, or a favorite quotation. To lighten this rather dry information, many authors have developed elaborate arrangements of text and symbols in their signatures.

Although widespread, signature files have not been entirely accepted by all Internet users. As a result, plays upon the signature file abound. One of the most succinct signature files, dutifully attached at the end of many messages, is "This is not a signature."

Chapter 3

The Electronic Library: Browsing with the World Wide Web

Is Microsoft a monopoly? Are black filmmakers disfavored at the Oscars? Is free verse poetry? You can begin to answer these and thousands of other questions simply by doing a search of the millions of resources available over the **World Wide Web**. The Web has become the single most significant Internet resource because of its tremendous flexibility and its incredible ease of use. How flexible is it? *All* of the other Internet resources described in the rest of this book—with the possible exception of e-mail—can be duplicated using the Web's protocol and interface. How easy is it? If you can point a mouse and click a button, you can use the Web.

Here's what you can find by searching on the World Wide Web for just twenty minutes (to learn how to search for Web sites, see pages 28–36):

Is Microsoft a monopoly?

Yahoo's News page on the Microsoft antitrust suit
http://headlines.yahoo.com/Full_Coverage/Tech/Microsoft/

Netsurf's page on Microsoft and antitrust
http://www.netsurf.com/nsf/v01/02/local/msft.html

"The Case Against Microsoft" by Dan Check
http://ourworld.compuserve.com/homepages/spazz/mspaper.htm

The Committee for the Moral Defense of Microsoft Home Page
http://www.moral-defense.org/

Are black filmmakers disfavored at the Oscars?

Offer to download a 21 March 1997 USA Today article on racism at the Oscars, from Web site search engine.
http://www.usatoday.com/

The official Academy Awards Web site
http://www.oscar.com/

An offer to buy transcripts of March 1996 episodes of the "Today Show," including the March 14 show when African American filmmakers appeared
http://www.burrelles.inter.net/services/toda9603.htm

Is free verse poetry?

A definition of free verse
http://www.english.upenn.edu/~afilreis/88/freeverse.html

The *Encarta* encyclopedia article on free verse
http://encarta.msn.com/

The Mining Company's English Literature Web site
http://englishlit.miningco.com/

These listings are just the tip of the iceberg. Many of the sites listed above include links to dozens more sources, all available instantly via the World Wide Web.

The World Wide Web

Now you know what the Web can *do;* here's what the Web *is.* Most simply, the World Wide Web is a communication system that delivers **hypermedia** built on the Internet's global network of computer networks. Hypermedia is an extension of **hypertext**. A hypertext document is text designed to be easily and richly linked to itself and to other hypertext documents. Hypermedia expands on that concept by including other media, such as audio, video, pictures, databases, and animation. Both hypertext and hypermedia can be incredibly powerful in the way they multiply the possible associations to a given piece of information. By connecting hypermedia documents to the amazing computing resources of the Internet, the World Wide Web magnifies that power exponentially.

World Wide Web documents are designed to be viewed using client programs called **browsers**. The two most popular browsers are Microsoft's Internet Explorer and Netscape's

Navigator (most people just say "Netscape" to refer to both Navigator and its newer cousin Communicator). Each file on the World Wide Web is assigned an address called a **Uniform Resource Locator** (**URL**—see page 9), which tells the browser the exact location of the file. Files are stored on Web servers which are equipped with software that enables documents to be linked and shared. The Web uses the **Hypertext Transfer Protocol** (**HTTP**).

The World Wide Web is revolutionary because it allows connections between documents regardless of their location. A single Web page might link to a sound file at an **FTP** site in Australia, a text file at a Gopher site in Europe, and a graphic file at a Web server in Idaho. In addition, most Web browsers now incorporate Internet technologies, like **Gopher** (see pages 54–55) and **newsgroups** (see Chapter 4), which previously demanded their own client applications

Browsing on the Web

So how do you visit a **Web site**? All you need to do is connect to the Internet (see Chapter 1), run your browser program, and type the site's URL into the "location" box of your browser. The site will appear on your monitor.

You can visit the many sites listed in this book in this way. You can also visit any site you may have learned about from another resource—your instructor, a book, an advertisement, or a friend. However, **browsing** is the way you find most of the information you'll need on the Web. With most Web browsers, this is done simply by pointing the cursor to a **link** (usually underlined text) and clicking. In the example in figure 3.1 below, to listen to the Spike Lee interview on racism in Hollywood, you move your mouse to point the cursor arrow at the text "Racism in Hollywood." The cursor arrow then turns into a pointing finger, as shown. This indicates that the text "Racism in Hollywood" is **hot**, meaning that something will happen if you click on it. Just click, and if your computer is properly equipped, you can hear Spike's comments on this issue. If your computer isn't set up for the type of sound file used on this site, you can download the software you need. **Downloading** is covered later in this chapter. This sample Web site also includes many other types of hot spots. Clicking the banner advertisement at the top of the page will take you to a site promoting the product. Below the banner ad is an **imagemap**, which can take you to many different places,

Figure 3.1: A sample page on the World Wide Web

depending on where you click on the image. To find out if a given area of a page is hot, just move the arrow over that space. If the arrow turns into a pointing hand, then clicking will transport you to another Web page.

Links are what give the Web its tremendous power. By connecting different media such as sound, text, and images, as well entirely different Web sites from around the world, they give you the power to create a media-rich environment that can't be duplicated in any other way. You can travel around the world and back simply by clicking on the links of the Web pages you visit. That brings up a potential problem. You could be reading a very interesting Web page about

Spike Lee, and then click on a link that discusses the Million Man March. Click on a link on that page, and you're at a site discussing the influence of Islam on the Civil Rights Movement. Interesting stuff, but weren't you writing a paper on racism at the Oscars? Fortunately, all Web browsers have a Back button, which simply takes you to the previous page you visited. Click again, and it takes you to the page before that. Decide you really do want to know about Islam and Civil Rights? No problem, just click on Forward until you return to that site.

An even more powerful feature offered by browsers like Navigator is the **Bookmark** command (Note: this book gives only Navigator commands; see table 3.1 for the Explorer equivalent). Bookmarks allow you to save the URLs of sites you've found to be particularly useful, so you can easily find them later. You can even organize your bookmarks into folders according to different research topics, and save your bookmarks to a diskette so you can use them on a different computer. In Navigator, you save bookmarks by first choosing Bookmarks from the Windows menu, then choosing Save as from the File menu.

Incorporating browsing into your research

Even though the Internet is a vastly different resource from traditional research sources, you can still follow the

Netscape term	Explorer equivalent
Location	Address
Bookmarks	Favorites
Save As	Export
Open Bookmark File	Import
Reload	Refresh
Back	Back
Forward	Forward
Stop	Stop
Monopoly	Innovation

Table 3.1: Netscape Navigator terms and their Microsoft Internet Explorer equivalents

same steps when using the Internet as a research tool as when you use a traditional library. You still need to narrow your topic, refine searches, and evaluate source materials. Here's a summary of how the Internet can be used with the steps in a traditional research project.

- **Finding a topic.** Surf the Web or perform keyword searches (see below) as you brainstorm on possible topics.
- **Narrowing and refining the topic.** Once a broad topic has been settled upon, running a more extensive set of keyword searches can help narrow and refine your topic.
- **Finding and evaluating sources.** When you have settled on a suitable topic, review the Web sites you visited while refining the topic. Determine whether they now offer new information or links, and investigate any promising new links. Perform additional keyword searches relating to all aspects of your project. Look for sites that refer to your sources (both online and other) to see what others have said about them.

Keyword searches

When you use a browser for the first time, you almost invariably will be pointed to a <u>search engine</u>. A search engine is simply a Web site which contains some sort of searchable index of the World Wide Web. You can type a word or set of words, and the search engine will present you with a list of sites that either include that word in their text, or have specified that word as a keyword.

While it may be easiest to simply perform your search with the search engine that comes up when you load your browser, you should realize that you have many more resources available. The only reason you see the search engine you do is because the search engine company has paid the company that makes your browser a lot of money. Different search engines have different features and work in different ways. It's important to identify the search engine that works best for the type of resources you're looking for.

Searching with Yahoo!

Yahoo! (*http://www.yahoo.com*), one of the oldest and most valuable Web searching tools, is not technically a

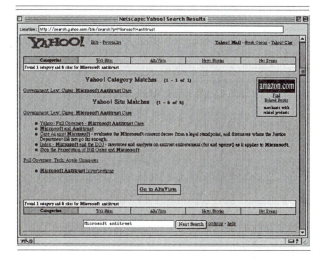

Figure 3.2: An example of a search using Yahoo!

search engine. That is, it does not simply search its database
for Web sites containing the words you specify. Instead,
dozens of workers actually visit thousands of Web sites and
place them in a hierarchical index, providing their own descriptions and even reviews of the sites they list. Yahoo! can
and does often reject a site from its index if it doesn't believe
the site to be a valuable or unique resource. (This doesn't
necessarily mean *useful:* Yahoo! lists close to a hundred "cam"
sites that simply show live pictures of some relatively benign
room or object deemed worthy of attention by bored computer hackers, such as the coffee pot in a research lab, or the
infamous Netscape Fish-Cam.)

Yahoo! offers two ways to search its listings. First, you can
click through its list of subject areas, which get progressively
narrower, until you get to a set of links to Web sites that interest you. This works well when you're narrowing a topic
but still aren't sure exactly what you're looking for.

Second, and more powerfully, you can type a search word
in the text box at the top of the screen. This allows you to
quickly reach the subject area that interests you. Figure 3.2
shows the results of such a search for "Microsoft antitrust."
Clicking on any of the links brings you to a site with more
specific information.

Yahoo!'s biggest strength—human indexers—is also its
biggest weakness. What a Yahoo! employee deems irrelevant

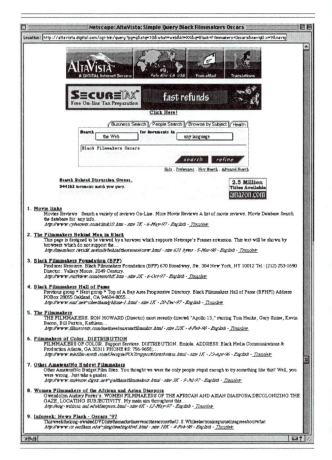

Figure 3.3: A basic keyword search using AltaVista

may be completely relevant to you. You have no way of knowing what's been left out by the human indexer. That's where the **robot search engines** shine—instead of relying on humans to catalog a select (if still very large) list of sites, robots try to automate the process and provide a way of searching the entire Web.

Searching with AltaVista

One of the most ambitious search robots, AltaVista (*http://altavista.digital.com*) attempts to catalog the entire Web by periodically visiting every known site and adding

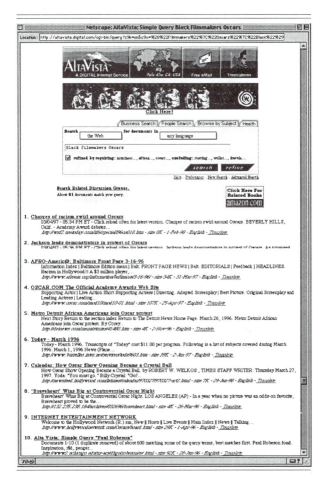

Figure 3.4: A refined keyword search using AltaVista

key elements of the site's text to its database. When you type in a keyword, it scans its database according to a predetermined set of rules and gives you a list of the results.

Figure 3.3 shows the results of one such search, using the keywords "black," "filmmakers," and "Oscars." This search returned over 300,000 Web pages! Unfortunately, because the search was performed by a "dumb" robot, many of the sites listed are not relevant to our search.

AltaVista offers a solution: the "refine" feature. Figure 3.4 shows the results of refining this search to require and eliminate certain terms from the search. Though this search returned "only" eighty-one documents, a much higher frequency of them were relevant to our research question. If your refined search doesn't generate the results you're looking for, you can always go back to the Refine screen and change its specifications, requiring or excluding different keywords until you get the results you're looking for.

Searching with Infoseek

Infoseek is one of David's favorite search robots because of its uncluttered interface and (usually) quick downloads. It works in much the same way as AltaVista, but offers a few additional options.

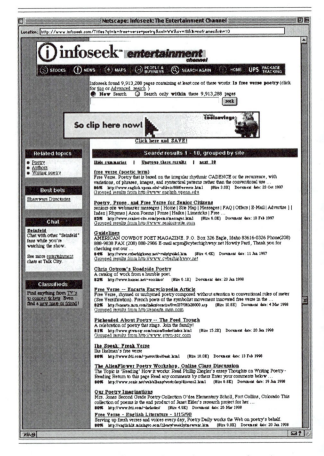

Figure 3.5: A basic keyword search using Infoseek

Figure 3.5 shows a basic keyword search using the phrase "is free verse poetry." The results were okay, but after noticing that many of the results were from the University of Pennsylvania's Web site, we tried searching just at U. Penn's site—an additional feature available with Infoseek (this was done by clicking on "grouped results for http://www.english .upenn.edu"). The result gave several additional pages which might have been difficult to locate by visiting the Web site itself.

Another useful feature of Infoseek is the ease with which you can search the results of a previous search. You can use this feature to search any Web site for a particular keyword. First, search for the complete URL of the site you're inter-

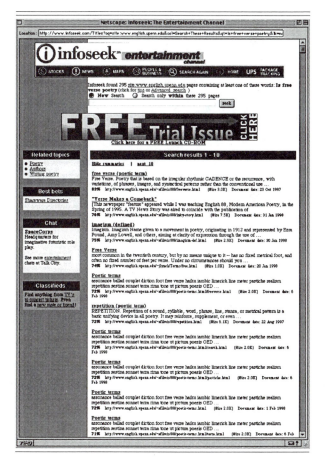

Figure 3.6: A Web site keyword search using Infoseek

ested in. Then, choose the "search these results" feature and type in the keyword you're interested in searching.

Searching with other services

There are literally hundreds of other search engines out there. Rather than give a lengthy description of each one, we simply provide a selection of their URLs with a brief note or two on the most popular engines.

Search engines (robots)

Excite
http://excite.com/
Attempts to avoid "<u>spam</u>" by ignoring keywords specified by Web site designers—success of this approach is debatable.

WebCrawler
http://webcrawler.com/
Easy to use, comprehensive. Gives just the Web page title— no descriptions.

Lycos
http://www.lycos.com/
Offers a "Top 5%" service which provides brief reviews of sites indexed.

Savvy Search
http://guaraldi.cs.colostate.edu:2000/
Allows you to search over one hundred engines simultaneously. A bit slow, but useful if you're having difficulty finding anything at all on your topic.

All-In-One Search Page
http://albany.net/allinone/

HotBot
http://www.hotbot.com/

Subject directory indexes

The Internet Public Library
http://www.ipl.org/
A subject directory created by librarians to mimick the organization of a library; very rationally and intuitively structured.

Library of Congress World Wide Web Home Page
http://lcWeb.loc.gov/
Search the entire Library of Congress catalog, an extensive online photo database, and more.

WWW Virtual Library
http://vlib.stanfordedu/overview.html
An index divided into hundreds of categories. Each category
is managed by a specialist, so categories are variable in quality, depending on the particular specialist.

The Argus Clearinghouse
http://www.clearinghouse.net/

Advanced Web searches

Boolean searches

Most of the engines for keyword searches allow you to use
some form of **Boolean** (logical) operators to modify search
strings. Employing these commands allows you to narrow a
search and to bring back a smaller number of **hits**. Hits are
simply listings of Web pages containing the search terms you
specify. Here are some of the basic commands—as it turns
out, the same commands you use for the various library
databases (such as the MLA online index).

Entering	Searches for
`pizza soda chips`	all sites containing the terms *pizza, soda,* or *chips*
`pizza AND soda`	only sites containing both the terms *pizza* and *soda*
`pizza OR chips`	either *pizza* or *chips* (note that *OR* is usually necessary only when combining Boolean operators)
`pizza NOT anchovies`	only sites containing the term *pizza* but not the term *anchovies*
`pizza*`	occurrences of the root within other words: pizzas, pizzacatto, etc. (a **fuzzy search** of *pizza*)
`"Chicago style pizza"`	only occurrences of all three terms together (a **literal search**)
`Mario Andretti`	Many search engines will consider any two capitalized words a **name search** and return only occurrences of the two terms together.

Boolean operators can also be used together. For example, the search pattern

```
racial OR sexual AND discrimination OR bias
```

would produce a list of Web pages containing any combination the following terms, in any order: *racial* and *discrimination, sexual* and *discrimination, racial* and *bias, sexual* and *bias* (but not any other pages containing only one of the terms, or combinations like *racial* and *sexual*).

Not every search engine uses Boolean operators in exactly the same way. Check the information provided at the site of the search engine to find out which functions are supported.

Using the Link command

Another useful command available on some search engines is the Link command. Suppose you want to know every Web site that links to the Microsoft Department of Justice Timeline. Simply type the following in the AltaVista search engine, then press the Search button.

```
link:http://www.microsoft.com/corpinfo/doj
/timeline.htm
```

AltaVista will list all the Web pages in its database that contain a link back to the Microsoft Timeline page. You can also use the Link command on Infoseek.

The Link command is a good way to find additional sources relevant to your topic, as well as sites that critique, analyze, or respond to a page you're interested in.

Searching for individuals

Many search engines and indexes, including Yahoo! and Excite, have "yellow pages" options that allow you to search for an individual's e-mail or physical address. The only problem with this function is that you usually need to know more than an individual's name in order to be sure you've got the right person. Suppose you type John Smith into Yahoo!'s yellow pages—you could end up with hundreds of listings.

In academic research, you may be interested in finding a faculty member at a college or university. In this case, it may be easier to go directly to that institution's home page and look for a "search" function. How do you find the institution's URL? Do a Yahoo! search.

Advanced browsing techniques

Search engines aren't the only way to locate information on the Web. Many times, you can get better results by exploiting the structure of a URL. URLs have several different components, and each component can lead you to a different place. Consider the URL for Microsoft's Department of Justice Timeline:

http://www.microsoft.com/doj/timeline.htm

The directory path consists of narrower and narrower subject divisions within the domain *microsoft.com*. If you want to find out additional corporate information about Microsoft, you could go to a search engine like Lycos and run an additional search, or you could simply delete the text *doj/timeline.htm* from the location box in your browser, and press Enter. That would take you to an index of the corpinfo directory, which contains many more links to Microsoft corporate information.

You can often speed up your browsing by taking advantage of the fact that large institutions usually have easily remembered domain names. For example, you could perform a Yahoo! search to look for Harvard University's Web site, or you could make an educated guess: just type http://www.harvard.edu in your browser's location box. In fact, both Navigator and Explorer will accept partial URLs—just www.harvard.edu works just fine. If you're looking for a corporate site, these browsers will even guess the server name and domain type correctly. Typing just microsoft will bring up *http://www.microsoft.com/*.

Other research sites

News sites

Just using search engines won't direct you to some of the most valuable sites on the Web. Internet search engines generally only index Web sites—not the information contained in databases located on the Web. Most major newspapers, news magazines, and television news networks have huge, searchable Web sites that allow you to find an immense array of documents on news events. News articles, photos, and other documents from these sites may not be indexed by the major search engines, so the only way to locate these documents is to go directly to the source. Many newspapers charge a fee for searching past issues, but one that doesn't as of press time for this volume is the *Seattle Times*.

Some newspaper and magazine sites

New York Times
http://www.nytimes.com/

Washington Post
http://www.washingtonpost.com/

Seattle Times
http://www.seattletimes.com/

Time Magazine
http://pathfinder.com/time/

Some television news sites

MSNBC
http://msnbc.com/

CNN
http://cnn.com/

ABC
http://www.abcnews.com/

Encyclopedia sites

Most encyclopedias on the Web charge a subscription fee of from five to ten dollars a month (for individuals). However, your institution may have a subscription already. If it does, you may be able to access the following Web encyclopedias free. Encarta offers a free abridged version that gives you a paragraph or two of text instead of the full article for each listing.

Encarta
http://encarta.msn.com/

Encyclopedia Britannica
http://www.eb.com/

Grolier
http://www.grolier.com/

Library sites

Most major learning institutions now have searchable indexes of their holdings on the World Wide Web. If your own institution has such a site, it may also give you access to additional resources available only to students and faculty at your institution, such as searchable indexes like *The Readers Guide to Periodical Literature, The MLA Index,* and others. If you don't find what you need on your own institution's site, try searching the catalogs from other institutions. You can often request holdings from other schools via your own library's interlibrary loan department.

Downloading helper applications

Some Web sites require **helper applications** in order for you to use the diverse media available on their sites. Most commonly, you may need a helper application to view video or hear audio files, or to view specialized Web sites incorporating animation or audio. In many cases, the site itself will provide a link to a site which allows you to download the helper application free of charge. For example, the Spike Lee interview shown on page 26 requires the RealAudio helper application in order to listen to the Spike Lee interviews. To download it, you would click on the RealAudio icon, and then follow the instructions posted at that site.

Generally, files you download will be **compressed**, meaning they are in a special format which must first be uncompressed with yet another helper application before they can be used. For Windows, most files can be uncompressed with WinZip, available at *http://www.winzip.com.* Macintosh files are generally compressed with Stuffit, available at *http://www.alladinsys.com/.*

Once you've downloaded a helper application, your browser will look for helper applications in a special folder on your hard drive, usually called Plug-ins.

Managing Web site information

As you begin to delve into your research topic, you'll begin to access a tremendous amount of material. It's temptingly easy to download everything about a particular topic. You need to choose selectively in order for your research to be effective. Skim a few online sources to get a sense of the broad context of your chosen research topic. Note those sources that you think will be most useful, and as you focus and narrow your topic, read these sources more carefully and follow links within them to new research materials.

You can quickly evaluate a source's usefulness for your topic by using your browser's Find command to look for a few key terms that you know are important to your topic.

Saving your work

Once you've determined which sources will be useful for your project, there are two ways to save your work. The first method is downloading an entire file to your computer. By choosing the Save as command from the File menu, you can save the actual text of any Web page to a computer disk. Saving images and other media is accomplished by clicking and holding the mouse button on the image (Macintosh) or clicking the right-hand mouse button (Windows).

Downloading text files is especially useful if there is a limit to the number of Internet-connected computers at your institution. You can take these files and read them on any computer, freeing up the Internet-connected computer for research by other students.

The second method assumes you will have access to the Web while you write your final research report. Simply bookmark any page you find relevant for easy reference later (see page 27). When you are writing, you can simply copy relevant text passages directly into your final document (with appropriate credit to the source—see page 99).

In either case, make sure you keep track of the original URL you accessed, as well as the date of access. Any time you quote an online source, it's a good idea to save the entire text of that URL. Since, unlike printed resources, Web sites can be instantaneously changed by their creators, you'll need to preserve your source in its original form to document it for your research.

Chapter 4

Usenet News

What are Usenet newsgroups?

Like private bulletin boards and commercial message sites, **newsgroups** are topic-specific sites of discussion and news distribution. The best thing about newsgroups is that you aren't just limited to reading messages others have posted. You can post your own message and engage other newsgroup members in conversation about an issue that interests you.

Your school will most likely be connected to **Usenet**, an enormous network of groups from around the world. The broad classification of Usenet contains thousands of topic-centered newsgroups organized hierarchically by name. The server at your school (the **news server**, or **news host**) collects and organizes the groups. You will access newsgroups with a **newsreader** (or news client), which provides an easy interface for reading, composing, posting, and downloading newsgroup messages.

Messages (or **posts**) displayed by the news reader are varied. Many come from other Usenet users like yourself. Others may be **news feeds**, or messages posted to a newsgroup by a wire service or other traditional news source. (Note that the word *post* can be used as either a noun or a verb.) The newsgroup messages form **threads**, consisting of an original posting and a series of replies on the same topic, usually with the same subject heading. The "news" at a typical Usenet newsgroup is a mixture of multimedia, personal postings, carefully crafted articles, and conventional news feeds. The groups not only distribute these topic-centered materials, but also fulfill an important social function by providing spaces where individuals can meet and engage in discussion.

At the moment, there are more than twenty thousand newsgroups online with an estimated ten million Usenet users. Perhaps this popularity can be explained by the way that Usenet accommodates such a diversity of topics and individuals, containing groups as different as *soc.adoption.parenting.pets.dogs.behavior*, *alt.barney.dinosaur.die.die.die*, *misc.activism.progressive*, and *soc.culture.kurdish*.

Newsgroups can be directed at audiences ranging from the local to the international (even extraterrestrial!). Many academic institutions, for example, will offer newsgroup services for affiliated courses and individuals. Most groups, however, are global in scope. For the purposes of our discussion, we divide groups roughly into three categories: news feeds, moderated groups, and unmoderated groups.

- **News feeds** represent the most familiar form of newsgroup information. Groups based on news feeds collect traditional news from wire services like the Associated Press and Reuters. Usually listed under the large CATEGORY or "Clari" newsgroups, these groups can be extremely useful for students doing basic research, providing instant access to a wide variety of current resources. Check with your instructor about the availability of the Clari news feeds at your institution.
- **Moderated groups** operate on the premise that messages posted to the group should be filtered through a moderator; therefore, not every message sent to a moderated list will be posted. Because messages which lean toward unsubstantiated personal rants are generally censored, postings to a moderated list often fall into the category of expert opinions or topic-centered articles. Many of these posts can be well argued and offer fairly knowledgeable insight into a research topic.
- **Unmoderated groups** are open to anyone and offer the best opportunity for viewing the diverse types of written interaction that can take place on Usenet newsgroups. Messages display varying levels of formality (ranging between scholarly articles and "chat") and often prompt substantial interaction. A posted message and subsequent responses (composing a *thread*) reveal a dialogue that often moves between a series of arguments and counter-arguments.

While these categories represent useful distinctions, most newsgroup discussions are unmoderated and involve a range of activities and types of messages. In some ways, the messages found on a newsgroup can be compared to those shared via a listserv (see page 18). The postings generally relate to a single topic and often provide insight and perspectives from knowledgeable individuals that can be easily incorporated as resources for student compositions. Some groups are more directly analogous to traditional print media, while others range toward personal opinion.

Although the audiences for newsgroup postings are quite broad, they are limited in other ways, primarily by the topic of each of the newsgroups. On an active group, the feedback that you may receive comes from informed readers who are knowledgeable about their subject matter—particularly beneficial when you are writing a research paper outside of your instructor's area of expertise. It can be helpful to post messages early in your research process to ask advice about sources or to get feedback about your ideas as they begin to take shape.

While individual newsgroups are limited in scope, with a substantial depth of topic in each, keep in mind that newsgroups in general are limited as a resource in other ways. While many knowledgeable Internet users can provide source information for an unlimited number of issues, overall the Internet underrepresents certain minority groups, economic classes, and even entire continents. Further, the English language dominates the Internet, and there are only a few non-English speaking newsgroups. Remember that newsgroup audiences may have important gaps in their demographic makeup which will necessarily have effects on the kind of information the Internet gives you.

How to use newsgroups

Most World Wide Web browsers now incorporate newsreading interfaces that coordinate the reading and composition of newsgroup posts (see Chapter 3). To point your browser to a newsgroup, type `news:` followed by the name of the newsgroup in your browser's location box. For example, to connect to the newsgroup *alt.activism* you would type `news:alt.activism`.

If you do not have access to the Web and a browser, you have other options for accessing newsgroups. The most basic news reading option is a client program residing on a remote Internet-connected machine. By **Telnetting** to an Internet account and activating a newsreading client, you can read and respond to newsgroup messages (see Chapter 5). A more user-friendly form of newsreader operates from the machines of individual workstations. These workstation clients allow users to customize lists of groups and offer searching, decoding, and other capabilities. Some common newsreaders are Newswatcher and Nuntius (for Macintosh) and WinVN and Trumpet News (for Windows).

Finding newsgroups on your topic

Many search engines on the Web allow you to search newsgroups. The most complete index of newsgroups is found at *http://www.liszt.com/news/*. You can also find newsgroups the old-fashioned way: when you open a news client like Newswatcher, a list of all newsgroups your news server subscribes to appears. Since most newsgroups have descriptive names, you can simply scan through the list until you find one that seems to interest you.

As you use more and newsgroups, you'll notice that some users post messages to more than one group. You can look at

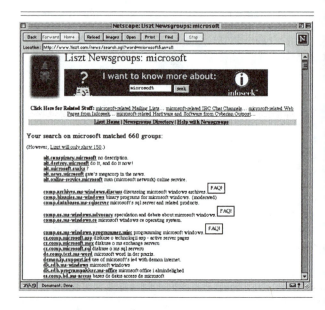

Figure 4.1: Results of a Liszt search for "microsoft"

the other groups members of your group are posting to in order to find even more resources.

With literally thousands of different Usenet groups to choose from, there is an excellent chance that you will discover groups discussing issues important to you and/or useful for researching class projects. At the same time, however, the overwhelming list of groups can be disorienting, and the process of searching through thousands of prefixed and suffixed names can be frustrating and time consuming.

Get accustomed to the idea of browsing newsgroups as a means of gathering materials for your research papers and projects. There are a number of topics for which Usenet will offer more (and more significant) materials than a traditional library. If you use Usenet groups to research extremely current topics or topics which are heavily discussed online— current Third World issues, environmental concerns, computer, or technology topics—you will very likely find much more material than you would searching through a library's collection of books and periodicals.

Also remember that newsgroups offer an extremely broad array of materials. You will be able to find not only well-written articles, but also important documents (for example, government legislation or official UN statements), as well as an array of opinions and perspectives on the issue. As we suggested above, this variety of information and multiplicity of voices can be addressed through a careful process of critical reading.

Saving your research

Keep in mind that newsgroups, by their very nature, are geared toward current events. Since the groups have limited storage size, newer postings displace older ones after a certain amount of time, or after the group has exceeded its size limitations. For researchers this means that the content of the groups is constantly changing, and a post that is available one week may be gone the next (especially on groups with heavy traffic). Unless you record them, resources can disappear from the group before you have a chance to get needed statistics or citation information. For this reason, always save and document any posts that you find particularly useful. If you are not sure what exactly you will need, it is always better to keep too much source information than not enough. It is a good idea to reserve a diskette solely for newsgroup resources. If you are using client software, you can archive the material you find online and "cut and paste" quotations into your papers once you have begun writing.

Posting to a newsgroup

Newsgroups closely intertwine the processes of research and conversation. You may begin using a newsgroup by gleaning information from it, but beyond just mining Usenet for existing resources, you should also consider posting questions and requests for information about your topic to appropriate newsgroups. Usenet provides a tremendous amount of expertise on even the most obscure topics. Of course, the people reading and writing these groups are not librarians paid to answer questions—they participate in the discussions for their own benefit and enjoyment. Group members will resent feeling obligated to answer obvious factual or historical questions. That is why it is crucial to spend time familiarizing yourself with the key issues, terms, and players in a debate before posting questions to group.

This is not to say that the newsgroup audience is unwilling to offer assistance. In fact, participants are surprisingly helpful and will often write long and thoughtful replies to student requests. In order to receive this help, though, you will need to compose your questions carefully. A confident but polite tone will go a long way towards eliciting useful feedback, but will not make up for a poorly conceived message. Do not generalize when composing questions, but rather be specific about what you already know on the topic, and what you need to know. Be careful with your use of important terms—the difference between "Croat" and "Croatian," for example, may be extremely crucial to some participants in a discussion about conflict in the former Yugoslavia. The best questions will spark debate on the newsgroup and allow the group members to offer assistance to the student while maintaining their existing level of conversation.

The communal resource: Benefits of newsgroups

Perhaps the greatest benefit of researching with newsgroups is their immediacy. One type of group offers news feeds from wire services like the Associated Press and Reuters, providing materials that appear in newspapers around the country. News is thus available as immediately as in a newspaper or on television, with the additional strength of near comprehensive coverage: anything the wire services produce is available online, whereas any particular newspaper has to curtail radically the amount of material it is able to present.

Although we have outlined distinctions between news feeds, moderated groups, and unmoderated groups, it can be more helpful to focus on the groups' messages and conversations. Besides news feeds, newsgroups fall roughly into two categories: "serious" and "chat." The serious groups, moderated or unmoderated, are more analytical and present a wider variety of opinions than the news feeds. Participants in these groups are often experts, and their opinions may be based on scholarly research of their own.

One benefit of serious newsgroups is that they offer significant information that is often absent from mainstream news sources, especially concerning international and Third World issues. For example, along with international news feeds on the January 1994 uprising in Chiapas, Mexico, newsgroups have provided the text of political pamphlets from the region. Thus current, locally produced information (unfiltered by publishers) becomes available to interested readers around the world.

The "chat" groups are less useful for serious researchers. Social message boards focusing on nonacademic subjects, groups like *rec.sport.unicycling*, *rec.music.beatles*, and *alt.aliens.imprisoned* will probably not be appropriate for your research project. Some chat groups can be useful, however. For example, the conversation on *alt.fan.tarantino* would prove interesting if your research paper considered the film *Reservoir Dogs*.

Reading critically

The volume of information available on newsgroups demands evaluation and critical reading skills. Because of the comparative absence of filtering processes like those more broadly employed in print publication, excellent materials are "published" on Usenet which would otherwise find space only in low-circulation, local presses, if anywhere. At the same time, because anyone with access to the Internet can post information and arguments to newsgroups, the material can often be untrustworthy.

Newsgroups are a paradox—a source of information both less reliable and more reliable than familiar items such as magazine articles. They may be less reliable because it is as easy to post (and thus "publish") off-hand messages with mistaken information as it is to post well-considered messages with viable arguments and accurate information.

Because the thoughtful and thoughtless messages appear side by side and in the same format, you need to distinguish potentially problematic messages from the two other broad categories of messages discussed above: postings from news feeds and messages from the "serious," more analytical discussion groups (which often make use of detailed research).

What is significant about Usenet is that most groups make little distinction among all these various types of messages. As a result, many newsgroups take on a kind of editorial objectivity which is quite different from that surrounding the printed source. When you read a magazine, for instance, you may notice that less "authoritative" material such as a letter to the editor is separated from the featured articles. Furthermore, you won't be able to see the many articles that were not selected for publication by the editors. In contrast, when you enter a thread of discussion in a newsgroup, you are instantly surrounded by a number of divergent voices and opinions, all pulling against one another in

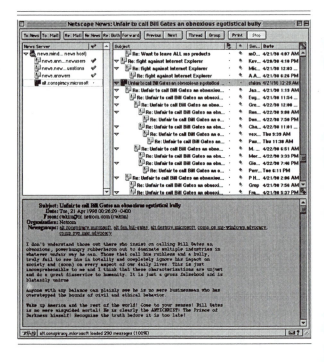

Figure 4.2: A newsgroup thread discussing Microsoft founder Bill Gates

a variety of ways. Through a careful process of critical reading, you might actually come to a fuller sense of the complexity of an issue than you might reach after reading isolated printed sources. The printed text by its very singular authority often cannot acknowledge the full range of other positions and voices that surround it in a public debate. Reading newsgroups, you may come to appreciate the extent to which both experts and hacks help define the terminology of a debate, its boundaries, its stakes.

In general, newsgroups facilitate the process of gathering various perspectives on the same issue. Messages found within the same thread often comment on, critique, or revise previous messages. The thread presents rich material demanding critical reading—that is, granting the writer as much credibility as possible while simultaneously keeping in mind opposing points of view and possible points of rebuttal. By looking at an entire thread in a newsgroup instead of a single article on an issue or two pieces which oppose one another, you find how many positions and assumptions are open to refutation.

Chapter 5

Telnet, FTP, and Gopher

Telnet

Telnet is a terminal emulation protocol: with a Telnet client you can establish a connection to a remote computer, almost like being at the machine's keyboard. Once connected, you can work with files in a specific portion of the computer's operating system (a **shell**), access files being shared by a server program, or activate other client programs that reside on the remote machine. You can download Telnet client applications like NCSA Telnet and Trumpet Telnet as **freeware** from a variety of sites or sometimes obtain them directly from your institution.

A Telnet connection is the most basic of all Internet functions. Before media like **Gopher** and the Web were available, researchers often used Telnet applications to connect directly to a site which offered a specific kind of database. An example of such a site is *info.umd.edu* at the University of Maryland. It offers an electronic archive of government documents (from the text of legislative bills to transcripts of presidential press conferences) and thus is still an excellent resource. While you might still use a Telnet application to connect directly to such sites, more and more archives are making their text files available through Gopher or the Web.

You have two basic options for using a Telnet client to access information on the Net. For example, when reading e-mail you could:

51

- Telnet to a shell on a mainframe and log on to the machine's mail server in order to read text files directly from the server.
- Telnet to a shell on a mainframe and activate a mail-reading client that resides on that machine. This remote client program will offer the reader an improved interface for managing mail. Note, however, that this interface is still limited by the simplicity of the Telnet connection.

If the only Internet technology you have access to is Telnet, you may still be able to reach World Wide Web files. Web clients can reside on remote computers and can be accessed with a simple Telnet connection. Here, for example is the interface for Lynx, a Unix-based text-only Web browser:

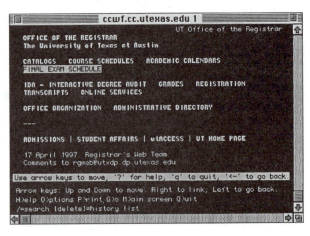

Each of the words or phrases in capital letters is a link; links are followed using the arrow keys, and other single keystroke options are available. Because Web pages contain multimedia elements, these Telnet connections give you severely limited access to the Web.

If you use other workstation client software, you will probably not make extensive use of Telnet applications or make direct Telnet connections yourself.

File Transfer Protocol (FTP)

File Transfer Protocol (**FTP**) is a basic means by which files—including text files, graphics, even applications themselves—are downloaded from and uploaded to central sites by users working at their desktop computers. Because FTP client programs can be used to download Internet software, they should be one of the first applications you obtain (probably from your computer services center). Transferring files can be a difficult process (though made easier by client programs), and we do not have the opportunity here to explain it fully. Some of the issues you will need to be concerned with are: knowing the address of a site which contains the materials you want, negotiating the directory structure on that site, choosing the right settings for downloading the files, and uncompressing these files to produce the resources you desire. Your institution may maintain its own FTP site with appropriate programs for your system.

You can find Internet client software at many FTP sites including the following:

- *ftp.utexas.edu* (Mac only)
- *ftp.dartmouth.edu*
- *wuarchive.wustl.edu*
- *ftp.ncsa.uiuc.edu*
- *ftp.stanford.edu*

Although file transfers can be performed with programs resident on institutional servers (often by typing `ftp` and an address at the prompt), we strongly recommend that you look into client software for this procedure—it will alleviate many of the difficulties involved in transferring files. Most of these applications also allow you to save site addresses, login names, and directory paths as bookmarks, so you can return to especially useful sites with one click of the mouse. Two common FTP client programs are Fetch (for Macintosh systems) and WS_FTP (for Windows systems).

Because files on FTP sites are sometimes **compressed** (rewritten in a way that consumes less memory) in a variety of different formats, you will probably need to have on hand several different applications for uncompression. The format used for uncompression will be indicated by the filename's suffix (the last part of the file name following a period, for example, *.sit*, *.tar*, *.zip*). If you do not have uncompression software, you will want to look for **self-extracting archives** (ending with the suffix *.sea*), which require no uncompression software; unfortunately, however, a lot of material is not compressed using this method. Uncompression software is available around the Internet for downloading, but tends to be shareware rather than freeware. You will have to compromise between your needs for downloading and the licensing fees you can afford. Speak with your systems administrator about the uncompression software you might need for particular files, as well as how to obtain and configure client software for FTP.

You may also use FTP for uploading files to a server, as, for example, in publishing World Wide Web documents. When loading files, make sure that HTML documents and any text files are sent as **ASCII text** or **text only** and that other media are transported as "binary" or "raw data." Also make sure that file names remain unaltered during the uploading process. You may need to turn off settings on the FTP client application which append extensions to the file names.

Gopher

Browsing on the Internet was first made possible by **Gopher**, a system of Internet protocols and directory structures that allows users to reach different machines worldwide and to view and search directory structures and available files. Along with a new ability to move fluidly from one site to another, Gopher provided a more user-friendly interface for file transfer protocol. Through Gopher, a user could for the first time easily browse the contents of Internet hosts and retrieve the files stored there. Computer science departments, libraries, and whole institutions quickly adopted this medium as a way to disseminate and share information. While use of the World Wide Web has almost fully supplanted Gopher, researchers at some institutions still use this technology.

A **Gopher server** (also referred to as a Gopherhost) stores and hierarchically organizes information which is read via a Gopher client application. A menu-driven Gopher interface (but without mouse support) can be accessed from most servers, with client software which operates from the server; on a Unix-based server, for example, this is done simply by typing gopher and the address of a host. With Gopher, these server-based client applications are fairly effective. Users will generally select items from a menu by entering the number that corresponds to the function they wish to perform. A Gopher client residing on a workstation, however, provides a much easier interface for searching and accessing documents and directories in **Gopherspace** (the universe of files accessible by Gopher clients). A file or application retrieved from a remote host is said to be **downloaded**.

Along with an easy interface, workstation Gopher clients offer several other advantages. You can create a **hotlist** of bookmarks pointing to Gopher sites you want to reference later. You also save text files, download and open graphic or sound files, and record a history of the files and directories that have been accessed since turning on the Gopher client.

Although Gopher functions have changed somewhat (especially with the ongoing absorption of Gopherspace by the World Wide Web), there are still three primary strategies for finding specific information using Gopher:

- **Targeting.** The user connects directly to a known address at a specific machine (a Gopherhost) and hunts through the site.
- **Tunneling.** The user accesses a number of Gopherhosts and explores their directories, which are organized both geographically as well as by subject. For instance, a user who was looking for information at MIT could follow the path "World/North America/United States/Massachusetts/MIT." The same user could search for information by subject, beginning in broadly defined directories such as "Libraries," "Government," or "Jobs." Since Gopher sites are organized hierarchically (much like the directory or folder structure of most personal computer operating systems), they can contribute structure to the wealth of information on the Internet. Each Gopher server organizes only the material on that local site, although researchers will become familiar with similar patterns of organization throughout Gopherspace. A user can move up or down through a Gopher site with some sense of direction.
- **Keyword Searching.** The user can use special functions of the Gopher client to search Gopherspace and retrieve files or directories containing specified words.

WAIS

WAIS, the Wide Area Information Search, is a powerful tool that helps users locate and extract information from a collection of documents. It is a long-standing public domain search engine, whose name is now something of a misnomer. The search covers a "wide area" in that it allows you to search multiple databases, but its area of coverage is narrower than more recently developed tools (like Veronica) that search multiple hosts worldwide. WAIS searches only a limited number of databases and requires that certain connections be established between the WAIS software and the text to be searched. WAIS searches are employed on Gopher sites, on Web sites, and on local databases.

Although (or perhaps because) WAIS covers a narrower body of materials than other searches, some of its search capabilities are more powerful. Many WAIS hosts will allow you to search the complete text of documents for your keywords, instead of just their titles or subject lines (as Veronica does, for example). Most WAIS applications support Boolean search strings, which will constitute the primary method for you to narrow your searches. For more information about the capabilities of WAIS and the material it covers at a particular site, look for a **readme** or **FAQ** file located on the site.

Veronica

Veronica is an index and retrieval system that can locate items on 99 percent of the Gopher servers around the world. As of January 1995 (the most recent figures available), the Veronica index contained about fifteen million items from approximately fifteen thousand servers.

To initiate a Veronica search, you must first connect to a site (located in cities like New York, Pisa, Cologne, and Bergen) that offers the service. Because such servers are often flooded with other users, a good strategy for trying to connect is to choose a host located in a part of the world where it is currently the middle of the night and fewer local users are likely to be logged on. Increasingly, however, even this strategy will not help. Some Gopherhosts now automate the login process, connecting you to the host with the least amount of traffic at the time of your request.

Once you log on to a Veronica host, you will be asked to enter a search string. Note that Veronica searches for words in titles of sources; it does not perform a full-text search of the contents of the sources.

If a Veronica search returns few or no sources, you can broaden the search without changing keywords. Veronica makes use of the asterisk wildcard; using it tells the computer to search for all occurrences of the root within other words (but the asterisk can only be used at the end of the root, not at the beginning or in the middle). This can be especially helpful, since the titles of Gopher files are often abbreviated to save space. A search for `envir*` will turn up not only titles using environment, environmental, environmentalism, and so on, but also a file named *environ.amazon.txt*.

If you are searching Veronica for a specific type of source, like image or text files, use the *-t* command followed by a number or letter for the source type. Some of the official file types include *O* (text files), *s* (sound files), *g* (GIF image files), and *I* (image files in formats other than GIF). For example, if you wanted to search for image files relating to George Washington, you would enter `George Washington-tI`. (When typing commands, leave no spaces between the items.) For further information about using these additional Veronica search commands, look for a readme or FAQ file in the search directory.

A Veronica search will produce a list of items very similar to WAIS results. The primary difference is that the items contained in it point to sites all over the world rather than those that reside on the same host. Research can thus be compounded by certain problems. With the duplication of materials on the Internet, different listings might actually take the user to the same resource, stored on two or more different sites. Additionally, certain sites may temporarily be down or too busy to allow connections. For these reasons, you should save the search results as a file so that you can return to those sites when the connections are re-established.

Browsing with Gopher

While the software you use to browse Gopherspace will probably be configured to use your school's host, you will be able to begin another Gopher session by entering an alternate Gopher address. Gopherhost addresses are machine names; therefore, they look much like the portion of an e-mail address following the @ symbol. For instance, you might connect directly to the host *Gopher2.tc.umn.edu* at the University of Minnesota, where Gopher was first developed.

If you already know the location of a site, you can search it out by moving through a sequence of geographical hierarchies. For example, say that you wanted to connect to the Gopher archive called the Latin America Network Information Center (sponsored by the Institute for Latin American Studies at the University of Texas). You would most likely select a directory called "World," after which you would move through a series of progressively narrower hierarchies. From the "World" directory you would first choose

"North America," then "United States," then "Texas," then "University of Texas at Austin." You would then choose "Colleges and Departments," then "College of Liberal Arts," then "LANIC." Note also that once you have located a useful site, using the bookmark feature of your client software can allow you to jump directly to that spot without having to follow the full path again. Although this process involves the techniques of tunneling, we include it in the discussion of targeting because the user is trying to reach a specific destination. For those who cannot enter a Gopherhost address directly, this method of targeting is the easiest way to locate a particular Gopher site.

Chapter 6

Real-Time Discussion: IRC and MU*s

What is Internet Relay Chat (IRC)?

__Internet Relay Chat__ (__IRC__) allows communication over the Internet as if in a conference call or over a CB radio channel. Using IRC, users can participate in topic-centered, real-time discussions over channels (or lines) that are roughly equivalent to radio frequencies.

Like the Usenet groups discussed in Chapter 4, the channels of IRC center on specific topics. In IRC channels, however, users can do more than participate on an existing channel; they can also quickly create their own channels. What makes IRC interesting is that multiple users around the globe can communicate in real-time with only a slight lag between exchanges. This almost instantaneous transfer of messages in IRC allows users to communicate in a way that resembles face-to-face conversation. Unlike e-mail or newsgroups, which are __asynchronous__ (i.e., there is an expected delay between messages) IRC lines allow for synchronous conversation.

This immediacy can present a problem: if your audience is not physically present, how can you convey the sorts of nonverbal signals (expressions, gestures, tone of voice, etc.) that people use in conversation? IRC allows users to send these signals with commands that represent the signal as something other than speech. Characters can use __emotes__, or descriptions of actions they are virtually "performing." For example, a user named Socrates could type `:listens intently`, and the text transmitted to other participants would read `Socrates listens intently`. In this way users can interact through writing—not only with conversational dialogue, but also by describing that dialogue.

A helpful way of looking at real-time discussions is as a hybrid that blends elements of writing and speech. A discussion in IRC reads a little like a manuscript of a play, in which a scrolling screen displays participants' names followed by a colon and then their dialogue or emotes. This sense of the theatrical is compounded by the fact that users are referred to as characters, and they often take on pseudonyms while online.

What are MU*s?

Like the IRC channels, <u>MU*s</u> offer spaces in which real-time written conversation and interaction can take place. MU* indicates a certain type of text-based, virtual environment, the first of which were the Multi User Domains (or "Dungeons"). MUDs were initially designed as a more sophisticated medium in which to engage in role-playing games like Dungeons and Dragons. Rather than use graphics to represent the fantastic worlds of these games, MUD participants could construct complex environments out of descriptive passages of text. These descriptions were placed on the Internet and scripted in a way which allowed multiple users to log on and be simultaneously present in the virtual space, adding an important interactive element to the games. Until recently these spaces have existed mainly as a forum for social interaction and gamesmanship. During the last few years, however, academics have started to see the value of these text-based environments and have begun to apply them to any number of scholarly projects.

MUDs gave birth to numerous different formats with names like MUSH and Tiny MUSH, each of which has slightly different protocols and scripting languages, as well as to the "MUD Object Oriented," or MOO. Rather than try to distinguish between MUDs, MUSHes, MOOs, and a host of other acronyms, we will use the term MU* to indicate a variety of these text-based virtual spaces. Because of the growing tendency for the more "academically oriented" of these spaces to be constructed using MOO scripts, we will provide examples mainly about MOO commands. Those details which do apply specifically to MOOs, however, can almost always be adapted with only minor variations to the other MU* formats.

Unlike the IRCs, the space of a MU* is a highly circumscribed environment in which the surroundings will dictate many of the user's options. Within the same MU*, a user could easily wander into and out of the reference section of a university library, a public hearing in a fourth-century BCE Grecian polis, a sci-fi nightmare, the second act of a Beckett play, the set of a movie, or just about anywhere else that someone might have imagined—all mapped out through textual descriptions. Rather than simply reading through the scrolling dialogue of an IRC channel, MU* users can move around, look at objects, and engage with their environment on a number of other levels.

MU*s and IRCs also free the class from some of the logistical constraints of the traditional classroom. A class that wanted to meet with students from another section or from another institution could log on to a MU* or an IRC environment. Similarly, an instructor could arrange to bring a number of guests from remote locations into the "classroom," or send students into MU*s and IRCs that are frequented by people outside of the class itself. As we have discussed in previous chapters, this kind of interaction with an expanded audience presents an important challenge to writers. You must shape your messages for your readership and be prepared to receive engaging and sometimes challenging response and feedback.

IRC channels and online discussion

Accessing and participating in IRC is a fairly simple procedure. If you are connected directly to a Unix-based network at your institution, for example, you might simply type irc to connect to the IRC server. Often, however, you will use an IRC client program on your workstation, which provides a much easier interface for your IRC sessions. Some common IRC clients are IRCle (for Macintosh) and MIRC (for Windows). These client programs will have the locations of IRC servers—often more than a hundred—pre-scripted for easy access. If you have been given instructions to connect to a specific IRC server, you can do so easily within the IRC client program. If not, you can experiment with different servers to see the types of channels that are available on each.

Once you are connected to IRC, you will need to distinguish between commands that you issue to the IRC server and the words that you wish to communicate to the group. The first character of a command is always slash (/). Some of the basic commands allow you to list or join channels or modify your nickname. Because the IRC clients facilitate conversation, simply typing a line of text and pressing Enter will send the message to all the users currently subscribed on an IRC channel. Your nickname will be attached to the text you write so that the message will automatically be ascribed to you. Thus, after a very brief introduction to the technology, you will find that the operation of IRC discussion is, for the most part, removed to the background.

IRC commands

- `/join #rhetoric`
  Joins you to an existing channel (here, *#rhetoric*): if the channel doesn't exist, creates a new channel.
- `/list`
  Lists all currently available channels. Be aware that listing them all will tie up your machine for several minutes. Type `/help /list` once you are online to manage this list.
- `/nick newnickname`
  Changes your nickname to whatever you type in place of "newnickname."
- `/names`
  Shows nicknames of users on each channel.
- `/who channel`
  Shows who is on a given channel.
- `/whois nick`
  Shows "true" identity of someone on a channel.

To create a new IRC channel, you simply join a channel that doesn't already exist. Choose a name obscure enough that it won't already be in use, but clear enough that the people you want to participate will recognize it.

Speaking, emoting, navigating, and building with a MU*

While MU*s offer a greater range of interactivity than the chat channels of IRC, they also require more time for learning the fundamentals of the medium.

As with e-mail and newsgroups, you can get to a MU* with a simple Telnet connection; this is the most basic way to connect to a server. Enter the **IP address** followed by the port number (usually either 7777 or 8888). For example, the address of Diversity University MOO is *moo.du.org 8888*. The interface provided by this kind of connection, however, is a bit cumbersome. For instance, the other users will scroll onto the screen as you compose new messages, breaking up the text you are trying to enter.

MU*s can also be accessed by activating a client application which resides on a remote machine. Though these these programs still rely on a Telnet connection, their interface allows a user to compose more easily and keep a record of the MU* session. Their operation may require knowledge of specialized commands.

Workstation client applications, such as MUDDweller or Mudling (for Macintosh) or MUTT or MudWin (for Windows), available by FTP as freeware, are the easiest way to log on to a MU*. Programs like this assist navigation, offer separate windows for composing messages, and provide easily retrievable transcripts. The simple connection and the rapid transfer of text are two reasons that MU*s have become so popular.

Many MU*s offer individual accounts to regular visitors with personalized names and passwords, and most MU*s have easy-to-use anonymous logins that allow first-time or infrequent users access to the MU*. If you plan to add any rooms or other features to the structure of a MU*, you will probably need to have an individual account on the server and permission from its system administrators.

Although some MU*s will require guests to use prefabricated identities, most will allow new users to configure temporary names and descriptions for their characters. By typing the command @desc me as a broad-shouldered guy carrying a Frisbee, a user named "bozo" would set his character description. Any other user who typed look bozo would see "a broad-shouldered guy carrying a Frisbee." You should take some time to construct a description of yourself as you wish to be seen. Define the gender of a character by typing @gender followed by male, female, or neuter; this will configure the gender of your persona with one of the traditional set of gender pronouns. You can usually see the full range of gender options on a MU* by typing @gender by itself. Daedalus MOO, for example, lets the user choose from a number of options: either (s/he), egotistical (I), plural (they), royal (we), splat (*e,h*), or even Spivak (e, em, eir, eirs, eirself, E, Em, Eir, Eirs, Eirself).

While we've talked about the ways that MU*s and IRCs challenge the idea of authorship through their electronic mesages, we don't want to suggest that they make a writer completely anonymous. In fact, one of the values of using IRCs, and probably to a larger extent MU*s, is that they allow students to develop alternative identities. You can experiment with online constructions of identity, as well as study audience reaction to various personas. For instance, the appearance of "an elderly, well-dressed African-American woman who would look equally comfortable lecturing in a university or serving food to the homeless with Food Not Bombs" is almost certain to change the flow of a conversation about affirmative action in institutions of higher learning.

The primary interaction that takes place on a MU* is text-based communication. The basic commands are `say` and `emote` (though these can usually be shortened to `"` and `:` respectively). The `say` command (`"`) attributes your name to any message you want to send. For example if your user name is "Athena" and you type in the line `Nobody knows you're a god on the Internet.`, everyone in the room (including you) will see the message `Athena says, "Nobody knows you're a god on the Internet."` The `say` command simply tells the MU* server to place your username and the word "says" in front of exactly what you type.

Similarly, the `emote` command (`:`) is used to attribute actions to you. It places your name in front of the text you type after the command. For example, the line `:rises in splendor and heads for the nearest temple.` will return the message `Athena rises in splendor and heads for the nearest temple.`

Though all interaction is thus narrated in third person, it is possible to communicate a wide range of thoughts, emotions, and actions. Since whatever you type after a say or emote command appears on the screen, you can include any number of sentences or any symbol you wish. The most obvious use of this feature is to "say" things with the `emote` command. By typing a message like `:says painfully, "I didn't know that was going to happen."` you will produce `Athena says painfully, "I didn't know that was going to happen."`

Emoting allows expression of any number of different attitudes, for instance humor or irony. To express certain subtle feelings, however, you must communicate through your writing rather than through emotes.

The basic MU* navigation commands are simply north, south, east, and west, but rooms in MU*s are often built to offer other dimensions of motion. A well-constructed room will inform a user about the possible options for movement and investigation. In fact, the details of a MU* environment can be quite elaborate and creative. Thus, building spaces on a MU* can require creative writing skills unlike those of the prose that may be stressed in the classroom. The well-worn dictum that descriptive writers should "show not tell" is especially pertinent for MU* environments. The skills you gain from writing precise descriptive prose for a MU* can be usefully extended to all your writing.

Basic MOO commands

Note: when you see *italic* text, replace that text with your own information.

look *object*	provides a description of the current room unless an object is specified
" *text*	allows you to "say" whatever you type in after the command
: *text*	makes your character "emote" whatever you type after the command
whisper "*text*" to *char*	speaks the message *text* only to the designated character *char*
read *name*	use to "read" newspapers or signs in MOOs
@desc me as *description*	provides a description of yourself for those who "look" at you
@gender *type*	gives your character the gender *type*
@help or help	gives more detailed information about MOO commands and their syntax
@dig "*name*"	creates a room
@desc *object* "*desc*"	describes a room or an object
@add-exit	creates an exit
@add-entrance	creates an entrance

`@dig direction` `to "room"`	links an exit and an entrance
`@leave`	defines what you see just before you go through an exit
`@oleave`	what others see when you leave
`@arrive`	what you see after you arrive in a room
`@oarrive`	what others see when you arrive in a room
`@lock`	prevents other users from entering a room or taking an object
`@nogo`	what you see if you can't go through an exit
`@onogo`	what others see if you can't go through an exit

`@create $object`
  `type named`
  `"name"`
	creates a new object of a given type ($note, $letter, $thing, or $container)

`@take`	picks up an object
`@take succeeded`	what you see when you take
`@otake succeeded`	what others see when you take
`@take_failed`	what you see if you can't take
`@otake_failed`	what others see if you can't take
`@drop`	drops an object
`@drop succeeded`	what you see when you drop
`@odrop succeeded`	what others see when you drop
`@drop_failed`	what you see when you can't drop
`@odrop_failed`	what others see when you can't drop

Chapter 7

Publishing Your Own Documents on the World Wide Web

Many people approach __HTML__ (__Hypertext Markup Language__) as if it is some horribly arcane and mysterious computer code that is only decipherable by a few gifted hackers. Believe it or not, publishing Web pages is really quite easy—and learning HTML is the easiest part of learning to publish effective Web sites.

Probably the best way to think about HTML is as a complicated typewriter. You can't produce a good essay, story, or report without knowing how to use the typewriter, but learning to use the typewriter doesn't necessarily mean you can write great poetry.

The best feature of your HTML typewriter is that as soon as you've produced your poem, essay, slide show, guidebook, or whatever, it's instantly available to anyone in the world with access to the World Wide Web—literally millions of people. This immense size of the Web's audience is also probably the most important thing to keep in mind as you create your Web site. Your audience is the global community of users of the Web, so your Web document should be easy to use for that audience—not the much more limited audience consisting of your classmates and instructor. Put yourself in the shoes of someone who hasn't taken your class, read the books you have, or even used the same kind of computer you're using. Your Web site should be accessible to them, as well as to your local audience.

There are six fundamental components of creating a good Web site. You'll notice that the actual HTML coding is just one of the six components. Most industry insiders believe it's much more difficult to find someone proficient at the "content development" phases—planning, authoring, and designing—than the "technical" phases—coding and posting.

The six components of Web site creation
1. Planning
2. Authoring
3. Designing
4. Coding
5. Posting
6. Publicizing

Planning a Web site

Most great writers are extremely well read. By the same principle, most good Web site designers have spent a lot of time surfing the Web, both to get ideas for their own sites and to learn from the mistakes others have made.

As you prepare to create your own Web site, spend at least an hour or two surfing the Web looking at sites similar to the one you're planning. If you've done research on the Web, go back to some of the sites you liked. As you surf, don't just pay attention to the content of a site—consider how easy it is to navigate. Is it easy to find the information you're looking for, or do you have to spend extra time seeking it out? When you need to visit a different portion of the site, are navigational buttons easy to find and understand, or do you have to scroll a long distance to the top or bottom of the page? Do pages load quickly, or do you have to wait for huge image or sound files to download? Are graphic images used appropriately, or do they distract from the overall message of the page?

If you make a list of the features of good Web sites versus bad ones, you'll begin to see how much thought and advance planning must have gone into the good sites. Among the most important considerations:

- How will the information on my site be organized?
- How much information should appear on each Web page?
- How will visitors navigate from page to page and around the site?

- What information should be presented graphically? What should be prestented in text? Should any other media be used? Audio? Video? Animation?
- How much memory is available for the site? What will the site's URL be?

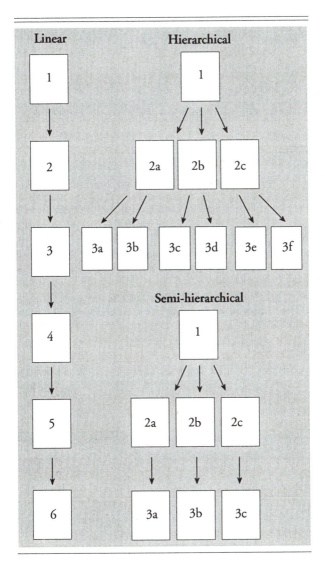

Figure 7.1: Common Web site organizational structures

Structuring your Web site

Deciding on an organizing principle for your site may be the most difficult decision you make as you plan your site. Unfortunately, it's also one of the first decisions you'll need to make. Making an outline of the material you want to cover should help. Also, look at figure 7.1, which gives three common organizational structures for Web sites. You should not feel constrained by these structures, but all have been used to create effective Web sites. One of the advantages of hypertext over traditional media is that it allows you to follow a non-linear organization for your document. However, be aware that visitors to your site can easily become confused if you do not provide a logical and easy to follow structure.

If you can't decide on one organization for your site, you can create alternate structures. For example if you choose the hierarchical organization in figure 7.1, you can also place a "next" link on each page that allows the visitor to read the pages in sequence: 1, 2a, 3a, 3b, 2b, 3c, and so on. Most visitors will expect to find a **home page** somewhere on your site, from which it is easy to navigate to any of the other pages on your site.

Once you've decided on an organizing principle, you'll need to determine how much material to include on each page. As you surfed the Web, you probably got some idea of the range of sizes for a single Web page. Some pages contain the equivalent of forty or more printed pages. Some contain just a single word. While any size in between can be appropriate, remember the constraints your users are operating under. While your university may have a high-speed connection to the Internet, most users are connecting over regular phone lines at speeds substantially slower. Just one small image may take up to a minute to download. While that may not seem long, consider the thousands of other options your visitors have access to. Sixty seconds is the length of two full-length television commercials. Is your Web site as exciting as Air Jordan and and the Energizer Bunny combined? A good rule of thumb is that a single Web page should take no more than fifteen seconds to download over regular phone lines. That's two or three pages of text, plus one or two small, memory-optimized graphics.

Presenting information on the Web

The Web allows you to present information in the form of text, images, and even sound, video, and animation. Text can be in tables, paragraphs, or even flying across the screen. Images can be photos, charts, and graphs designed for ornamentation or information. As you consider how to present information, remember that each method has strengths and limitations. Some of these are summarized in table 7.1. The table is arranged according to increasing memory requirements. It's also important to note that each medium requires specialized software to produce. Though text and image-editing software is relatively abundant, software for animation, audio, and video can be quite expensive.

The media you choose will, of course, depend on your topic. If your Web site analyzes the songs of various birds, for example, then audio will be an essential component. However, if it considers only the poetry of Mary Wroth, then text will likely be the most important medium for your site.

Since text is the "cheapest" in terms of computer memory and time it takes to create, most Web sites contain a lot of text. But if the purpose of a site is to display a collection of photos or original artwork, for example, a lot of text may simply get

Type	Advantages	Limitations
Text (TXT)	Uses least memory. Easily printed and saved.	Can be dull, unattractive.
Images (GIF, JPEG)	Uses moderate memory. Stable on many different types of computers.	Can be overused. Can take a lot of time to prepare.
Animation (GIF)	Uses moderate memory. Useful when well done.	Can be annoying. Usually in poor taste.
Audio (WAV, AU)	Only way to present certain types of data.	Uses substantial memory. Can be very annoying. No Internet-wide standard for file format.
Video (AVI, MOV, MPG)	Only way to present certain types of data.	Uses most memory. No Internet-wide standard for file format. Very slow on almost any platform.

Table 7.1: Advantages and limitations of different information types

in the way of the message you're trying to convey. Whenever you choose a particular medium for your Web site, make sure you've made an informed decision about using it.

Authoring your site

Once you've made the important decisions about what information you will present on your site and how it will be presented, the next step in the process is authoring. **Authoring** is an awkward word, but it is probably the most descriptive term for the process of creating the content material that will be presented on a Web site. Authoring is roughly analogous to writing the manuscript for a book, the script for a play, or taking the photos for a public exhibition. As a content author, you create or obtain from other sources all of the information that will be presented on your site.

Crucial to the process of authoring a Web site is considering the experience that visitors to your site will have when they visit. David Siegel, author of *Creating Killer Web Sites*,

Figure 7.2: Many Web authors like to create a complete atmosphere, much like a themed restaurant.

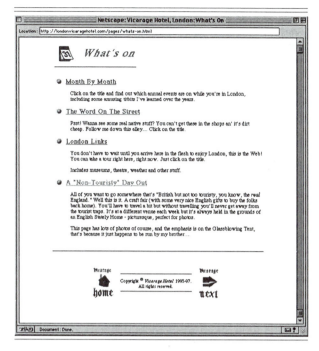

Figure 7.3: Some Web authors prefer to style their sites after a conversation between close friends.

suggests that the experience of visiting a site should be like going to a restaurant, where visitors first see an enticing entrance, which leads them to a host, who guides them to a table, where they are presented with a tempting menu of choices to select from (figure 7.2). In contrast, Jim Rhodes of Deadlock Design feels a Web site is more like a place for one-on-one conversation. Since visitors are typically sitting by themselves in front of a lonely computer screen, Rhodes contends, a Web site should talk to them like a close friend—chatty, casual, with lots of inside information (figure 7.3).

Clearly, many different approaches to Web authoring have been successful; however, all successful site authors carefully consider the experience of the visitor as they create content. What might your potential visitor be looking for? What is the clearest, easiest, most efficient way to give it to them? What information will visitors bring with them? Are there any existing Web sites that provide background information that might be useful to your visitors? What tone and style will be most useful and appealing for your visitors—formal? casual?

irreverent? Are people clamoring for the information your site will provide or is the information unavailable elsewhere? If so, they might be willing to tolerate long downloads for your information. If not, you'll need to impress them with high-quality writing, crisp images, and quick downloads.

Content authoring clearly requires proficiency in whatever medium you're producing: writing for text, artistic ability for images, musical ability for sounds. It also requires varying degrees of computer skill, depending on the medium. Text merely requires the ability to operate a word processor. Images might require the mastery of one or more **image editors**. An image editor is a computor program designed to create and modify images. The most common image editor for Web applications is Adobe Photoshop. However, almost every progam that can create an image can save it in a Web-compatible format. Ultimately, you'll need to create a **GIF** or a **JPEG** image, so make sure whatever image editor you use supports one or preferably both formats. If you're planning on using photos on your Web site, you'll either need access to a **scanner** to convert the photo into a computer file, or you'll need to use a commercial film processor that offers **Photo CD** service.

While it's beyond the scope of this text to discuss the technical aspects of image creation, we can offer a few pointers.

- Keep images as small as possible. Most users have small monitors: 640 by 480 **pixels** is most common.
- Use as few colors as possible. The more colors, the more memory your image uses.
- Only include relevant images. Since images take time to download, make sure they are relevant to your discussion.
- On the other hand, don't skimp on images. Users will quickly tire of page after page of text.
- Make sure you have permission to use borrowed images. Remember, copyrighted images cannot be placed on the Web without permission. If you can't get permission to use a graphic that's already on the Web, you can always include a link to the existing Web site.

Designing your site

Once you've created the content that will appear on your site, you're ready to design the site itself. Perhaps the easiest

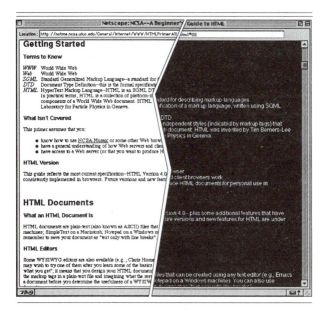

Figure 7.4: **The two faces of a Web site. Depending on
how you set your browser, the same Web site
can appear very different.**

way to do this is simply to sketch it out with pencil and
paper. What will visitors see when they arrive at your site? A
table of contents? Introductory text? A tone-setting photo?
Where will visitors click to get to the main content pages of
your site? Will each page include navigational links users can
click on to access the main parts of your site, or will visitors
be forced to visit each page in sequence? What will your
headings look like? Where on each page will images appear?
Now is the time to decide on the details of how your site will
unfold to visitors.

The way you make these design decisions is up to you.
You may use pencil and paper, as described above. If you're
like Web design master David Siegel, you could create a layout of each page on your site using Adobe Photoshop. Or
you can use your word processor's formatting capabilities to
generate the basic look and feel of your site.

Once you've made these critical decisions, you're ready to
take the final step before actually posting your site on the
Web: coding in HTML.

HTML: The language of the Web

How do you create a file that is publishable on the Web? Take the text you've created in any word processor, save it as "text.html", and load it onto a Web server. Most browsers will read simple text only files and display them the same way any Web page is displayed.

Figure 7.5 shows the results of saving a raw text file and opening it in a Web browser. The first thing you'll notice is that your text's all there, but the formatting is gone. Your title is not centered, paragraphs aren't indented—in fact, the whole thing is one big paragraph. That's the first lesson to learn about HTML—your browser will strip away all the formatting you use in your word processor and replace it with plain, unformatted text. Don't worry, there's a way to add this formatting back to your document. In fact, HTML allows you to do much more than that. Throughout this section, we'll gradually build a small Web page starting from a simple text file. When you're done, you'll be able to build a similar Web page yourself.

Figure 7.6 shows the same file with a few basic formatting commands added. As you can see, adding the formatting commands has made our text file look much worse, but it has made the actual document visitors will see much more attractive. In HTML, all the formatting commands are called **elements**, which in turn are made up of **tags** enclosed in angle brackets. By examining the example shown here, you can notice a few things about HTML tags:

- All tags must be enclosed in angle brackets
- Though it's not required, tags are easier to locate in your HTML file if you type them in ALL CAPS.
- Most elements require an opening tag (for example <B> for bold text) and a closing tag to signal the end of that element (in this case, </B>). All closing tags start with the slash character (/). The most important elements that don't require closing tags are <P> (paragraph),
 (new line), <HR> (horizontal rule), and <IMG> (image).
- Some tags take **attributes**, which give additional information about how the tag is to be applied. For example, here the <H1> tag also includes the attribute ALIGN="Center". This combination tells the browser to not only display the text as a first-level heading, but also to center that text.

A Century of Trustbusting:
What Can It Tell Us Today?

In the 1890s, American industry was dominated by a few Titans, sometimes derogatorily termed "Robber Barons." Preeminent among these was the Standard Oil empire, presided over by John D. Rockefeller.

Now in the 1990s, industry is again dominated by a few charismatic Titans. The most powerful and wealthiest of them all, Microsoft CEO Bill Gates, has been called both an innovator and the Antichrist.

Standard Oil was broken up as a result of the Sherman Anti-Trust Act. Today, Microsoft may soon suffer the same fate.

This Web site explores connections between the American industrial landscape

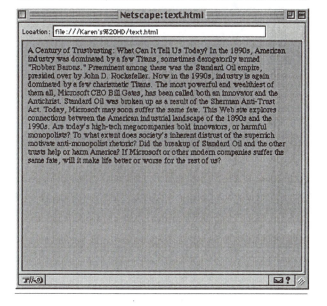

Figure 7.5: The text you type in a word processor and the same text displayed on a Web browser

```
<H1 ALIGN="Center">A Century of
Trustbusting</H1>
<H2 ALIGN="Center">What Can It Tell Us
Today?</H2>

In the 1890s, American industry was
dominated by a few Titans, sometimes
derogatorily termed "Robber Barons."
Preeminent among these was the
<B>Standard Oil</B> empire, presided over
by <B>John D. Rockefeller</B>.<P>
Now in the 1990s, industry is again
dominated by a few charismatic Titans.
The most powerful and wealthiest of them
all, <B>Microsoft</B> CEO <B>Bill
Gates</B>, has been called both an
innovator and the Antichrist.<P>
Standard Oil was broken up as a result of
the <B>Sherman Anti-Trust Act</B>. Today,
Microsoft may soon suffer the same
fate.<P>
```

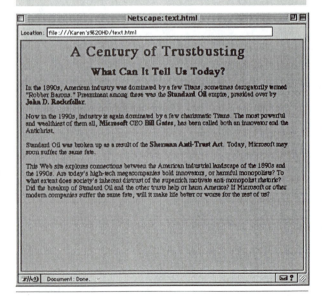

Figure 7.6: Text with some basic HTML formatting
displayed on a browser

In this example, we created two levels of centered headings, using the <H1> and <H2> tags combined with the ALIGN="Center" attribute. You can specify up to six levels of headings (<H1> through <H6>, but hopefully you'll never need more than three), and you can also specify Left, Right, and Justify with the ALIGN attribute.

We also placed several important terms in boldface type using the bold tag, <B>. You can also create italic (<I> . . . </I>), underlined (<U> . . . </U>), and larger or smaller type (<BIG> . . . </BIG>, <SMALL> . . . </SMALL>).

Paragraphs are specified in HTML using the <P> tag. Most browsers will place an extra line of space between each paragraph. If you don't like this look, use the <BR> tag to take you to a new line with no space.

Adding structure, links, and images

You now know how to make a passable Web page using HTML. However, this page still has a few flaws. First, it doesn't contain any links to the rest of the Web, or even to other pages on this site. It's rather uninteresting visually, with a dull gray background and no images at all.

In figure 7.7, many of these problems have been addressed. The document has now been structured as a formal HTML file. The HTML structure tags are <HTML>, <HEAD>, and <BODY>. <HTML> and </HTML> tags should surround the entire document. Then the document should be split into two parts, the Head and the Body.

The Head contains descriptive information about the HTML document. In this case, the only information is the Title tag, which causes the title to appear in the browser window framing the document. If you don't include a Title tag, the name in the browser window becomes simply the file name (see figure 7.7).

The Body tag surrounds the rest of the file and can have several attributes. In this case, we've specified white as the background color, green as the link color, red as the color for links the visitor has already visited (VLINK), and black as the text color. In addition, you can specify a background image to be displayed behind all text and images in the document. What you can't see in the figure is that the file name has also been changed to *index.html*. This is the standard file name for home pages. The benefit of using *index.html* as your file name is that you don't have to type it in the location box to point your browser to the file. Just type the domain name and any subdirectories, and your browser will automatically open *index.html*.

```
<HTML>
<HEAD>
<TITLE>A Century of Trustbusting</TITLE>
</HEAD>
<BODY BGCOLOR="White" LINK="Green"
VLINK="Red" ALINK="Red" TEXT="Black">
<IMG SRC="banner.gif" HEIGHT="119"
WIDTH="500" ALT="A Century of Trustbusting:
What Can It Tell Us Today?">
<P>
<HR>
<P>
In the 1890s, American industry was
dominated by a few Titans, sometimes
derogatorily termed "Robber Barons."
Preeminent among these was the <B>Standard
Oil</B> empire, presided over by
<A
HREF="http://voteview.gsia.cum.edu/entrejdr
.htm">John D. Rockefeller</A>.<P>

Now in the 1990s, industry is again
dominated by a few charismatic Titans. The
most powerful and wealthiest of them all,
<A
HREF="http://www.microsoft.com/corpinfo/">M
icrosoft</A> CEO
<A
HREF="http://www.vanderbilt.edu/Owen/froeb/
mgt352/MrBill.html">Bill Gates</A>, has
been called both an innovator and the
Antichrist.<P>

Standard Oil was broken up as a result of
the
<A HREF="http://k7moa.gsia.cmu.edu/antitrst
.htm">Sherman Anti-Trust Act</A>. Today,
Microsoft may soon suffer the same fate.<P>
This Web site explores connections between
the American industrial landscape of the
1890s and the 1990s. Are today's high-tech
megacompanies bold innovators or harmful
monopolists? To what extent does society's
```

```
inherent distrust of the superrich
motivate anti-monopolist rhetoric? Did the
breakup of Standard Oil and the other
trusts help or harm America? If Microsoft
or other modern companies suffer the same
fate, will it make life better or worse
for the rest of us?<P>

<P ALIGN="Center"><A
HREF="standard.html">The Standard Oil
case</A> - <A HREF="social.html">Social
reactions to billionaires</A><br> <A
HREF="mscase.html">Microsoft antitrust
case</A> - <A HREF="outlook.html">The
outlook for the future</P>
</BODY>
</HTML>
```

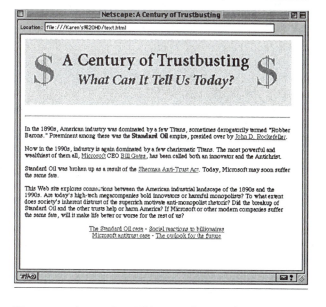

Figure 7.7: A complete HTML Web page along with the
text file required to generate it. Note
especially how the <A> tag is used to create
hot text.

Links

One of the most powerful features of HTML is the ease with which documents from all over the world can be linked together. The standard format for an HTML link is:

```
<A HREF=URL>Hot Text</A>
```

In this case, you'd substitute in the URL of the document users will see when they click on "Hot Text." In figure 7.7, "John D. Rockefeller" is hot, and when visitors click on that text, they will be transported to a biography of Rockefeller at *http://voteview.gsia.cmu.edu/entrejdr.htm.* Several links have been added to our sample Web site. Look closely at them to see how they work. Note that the links at the bottom of the page link to **local** files. In this case, the link only requires the file name, and that's all you should provide. That way, while you're coding your Web site, you can keep all the files on your own local workstation. When you're finished coding, you can post your site to the server, and assuming you keep all your files in the same directory, all the links will still work. If you had used absolute references when building your site, they wouldn't work after the files were uploaded.

Images

We've added a banner headline to our document instead of relying on the `<H1>` tag to provide formatting. This sort of simple artwork can add a bit of flair to a page. Many site designers use image files not only for document headlines, but also for subheadings, to assure a uniform look on different users' systems. If we could have obtained permission, we also probably would have included photos of Bill Gates and John D. Rockefeller, to personalize the page even more. Here is the general format for placing an image in a document:

```
<IMG SRC="imagename.gif" HEIGHT=pixels
WIDTH=pixels ALT="Text appearing if user can't
see the image">
```

Look at figure 7.7 to see how the words in *italics* get modified for a specific image. Note that in order for your browser to recognize a file as an image, the filename should always end in *.jpg* or *.gif* to indicate the type of file it is (see page 84 for a discussion on how to prepare images for the Web). In almost every case, the HEIGHT and WIDTH you specify should be the same as the actual dimensions of the image file you created. Otherwise, the image will look distorted and ugly.

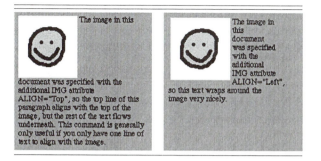

Figure 7.8 Results of different applications of the ALIGN attribute for images

The ALT text is especially important because many users do not have graphical monitors, and others with slow Internet connections will turn the images off on their browsers. It also provides the only information of any kind blind visitors will get (unless your site includes audio files).

Another important attribute of the <IMG> tag is ALIGN. Please note that ALIGN works differently for images than it does for the <P> and <H1> tags. With images, the ALIGN attribute specifies how the text in the document will wrap around the image. "Left" and "Right" are the most valuable, because they allow the accompanying text to wrap around the image, as in figure 7.8. You can also specify "Top", "Bottom", and "Middle", but these are of limited use because they only place one line of text next to the image.

You cannot use the ALIGN attribute to center an image horizontally on the page. The only way to accomplish this is by surrounding the <IMG> tag with a <P> . . . </P> tag, as follows:

```
<P ALIGN="Center"><IMG SRC="imagename.gif"
Height="pixels" WIDTH="pixels" ALT="Centered
Image"></P>
```

Considerations while you're coding

As you code your Web page in HTML, it's easy to check your code to see if it's working. Just remember to save your HTML file as text. Then you can open the file in your browser and see what it looks like as you work. If you know you've made a change in the text file, but it doesn't appear in

your browser, just click on Reload and the page will be updated to include your new coding.

It's probably a good idea to keep both your browser and
text editor open while you work, so you can easily go back
and forth between the two and correct mistakes as they come
up.

Preparing images for the Web

Images are what separate the professional Web designer
from the millions of casual Web users who've managed to
post up their own Web pages. You can spot a novice Web
designer in a minute by simply observing how efficiently
he's used images. A 148K image on a home page is a sure
sign of someone who doesn't know what he's doing. Experts
know how to use memory more efficiently, so even large images take up less than 20K. (A **kilobyte**, usually abbreviated
K, is simply a unit of measure of memory for computer
files—on the Web, smaller is better.) A 148K file might take
over a minute to download over slow phone lines. By that
time, your visitor has probably surfed on to a site in
Tanzania.

The key to making memory-efficient image files is under-
standing how computers save memory. The two major file
formats save memory in two different ways: very basically,
GIF files (pronounced "jiff") save memory by limiting the
number of colors in a document, while **JPEG** files (pronounced "jaypeg") save memory by limiting the resolution
of a document. Depending on the particular image, either
format can produce more savings. Again speaking very gen-
rally, GIF files work better for line drawings or typographical art consisting of one to twenty distinct colors. JPEG files
work better for photographs or paintings with lots of details
and thirty or more distinct colors.

While it's beyond the scope of this book to give specific
instructions on creating images, the following should help
you optimize your images for the Web once you've created
them. Our instructions are based on Adobe Photoshop, but
most image-editing programs have similar commands.

Optimizing GIF files

Once you've created your image, make sure it's in Color
RGB format. You can specify this by selecting RGB Color

from the Mode menu in Photoshop. Then make your image the size you want it to appear on your Web page (in pixels) using the Image Size command on the Image menu. Remember that most users have 640 × 480 monitors, so you certainly won't want to specify an image size larger than this. Write down the dimensions of your image in pixels—you'll need this when coding your HTML.

What comes next is the key to optimizing your file. You're going to change your file format from RGB to Indexed Color. With Indexed Color, you can specify the number of colors your document uses. The fewer colors, the less memory your image consumes. With many images, you can get the number of colors down to less than ten with no significant loss of resolution. Try it. Just select Indexed Color from the Mode menu, type the number of colors you want, and press OK. Start with a small number, like 10. If the result looks great, you may be able to do better. Select Undo from the Edit menu and try a smaller number. Repeat these steps until you find the smallest number of colors that produces an acceptable image. Then choose Save As from the File menu. Type a file name ending in .gif, and select Compuserve GIF as the file format. Make sure you write down the file name so you have access to it while you're coding.

Optimizing JPEG files

Optimizing JPEG files is done slightly differently, because the memory optimization process occurs while you are saving the image file itself. Once you've made your image the size you want, choose Save as from the File menu. Type a new name ending in .jpg and select JPEG as the file format. You can then choose from four different image quality settings. The lower the image quality, the less memory the image consumes. Even the lowest setting produces surprisingly good results. You can then look back at your image and decide if the loss of resolution is acceptable. It's important to save your original image file as well as the JPEG file in case you want to edit the file later or you decide the resolution you've chosen is unacceptable.

If you need to include a very large (over 50K), detailed image on your Web site, you should consider making two images—a small placeholder image and the full-size original image. You can code your HTML so that when users click on the small image, the larger image is downloaded onto their browser:

```
<A HREF=largeimage.jpg><IMG SRC=smallimage.jpg
HEIGHT=pixels WIDTH=pixels ALIGN="Left">Click to
download a larger image</A>
```

File management while coding

As you code your Web site, you will begin to generate a considerable number of files. The most important rule of Web file management is to keep only files destined for your Web site in the directory containing your HTML and image files. Any files such as non-HTML word processing files, non-GIF or JPEG image editor files, or other data you may have used to create your Web site should be kept separate from your Web files.

If the number of distinct files required for your site exceeds thirty, you may want to consider adding a directory structure to your site. For example, if you have a hierarchical site with four major subdivisions, you may want to create a subdirectory for each of the subdivisions, each placed inside the main directory (which contains only the files for your home page).

Relative vs. absolute URLs

Once you reorganize your site to include subdirectories, the way you link to pages on your own site must change. When linking to an outside Web site, you always need to use the complete URL (the **absolute URL**). However, when linking to a file located in a subdirectory of your own site, you should use the local or **relative URL**. This is a partial URL that takes advantage of the fact that your browser already "knows" the URL of the current Web page. The simplest relative URL is one you're already familiar with—just using the name of the file for URLs in the same directory. To link to a file in a subdirectory of the director you're in, use the following syntax:

```
<A HREF="subdirectoryname/file.html">hot text</A>
```

Once you're in a subdirectory, getting back to your site's main directory without resorting to absolute URLs requires another bit of syntax. The notation ../ means "the directory containing the current directory" and can be used to go "backwards" in the current directory tree. Thus, if your file is in a subdirectory, and you'd like to link back to the main page in the directory containing it, use this syntax:

```
<A HREF="../index.html">hot text</A>
```

DON'T use
```
<A HREF="parentdirectoryname/index.html">hot
text</A>
```
(this syntax will NEVER work)

Because keeping track of relative references can be difficult, many professional Web designers keep all their files in the same directory even if the total number of files exeeds one or two *hundred*. At some point, however, you'll simply have to subdivide, so learning relative notation is essential for proper file management.

Posting your site to the Web

After you've gotten your site to work perfectly on your local computer, it's time to post it to your institution's Web server. Up until now, you've been the only person with access to your site. Posting your site on the server means that everyone in the world with access to the Web can see your site.

What the server does

Serving files involves two major activities: 1) overseeing the behind-the-scenes operations of the Web server, including setting up form and imagemap routines, and running software which provides the proper protocol for sharing files on the Web, and 2) managing directory structures and files which reside on the Web server. Organizing your files and uploading them to a server may require some extra time and energy, especially if you are uncomfortable with the various technologies. Whatever your level of technological knowledge, we recommend that you coordinate with your Web administrators as you work through the various tasks involved in serving your files.

Usually your computer services center or some other institutional entity will be responsible for the operations of the Web server, so you will probably not be involved in the first of these two activities (if you do need information about the server-side operations of the Web, see *http://Web66.coled.umn.edu/Cookbook/*). Some institutions will provide students with individual accounts for Web building, but in many cases, the instructor will be responsible for managing files for the entire class.

Uploading files

There are two main ways to upload your files to your server. If your computer is connected directly to your campus network (for example, a Windows NT network), you may be able to copy your files directly to the server the same way you do locally. Otherwise, you'll probably be using an FTP client (see Chapter 5). You may be able to load all of your directories at once, depending upon your FTP client. Otherwise, you will need to place files on the sever individually. In any case, check that the final organization of the directories and files that you load to the server mirrors the structure of any projects developed locally. Additionally, when loading files, make sure that HTML documents and any text files are sent as ASCII text or text only and that other media are transported as binary or raw data. Make sure that file names remain unaltered during the uploading process. Finally, after you have placed files on the server, you should check the links with a browser to ensure that nothing has gone wrong.

Publicizing your site

Once you've posted your site, you want people to visit it, right? Otherwise, you might as well have left it on your local computer. Fortunately, there are many free and easy options for publicizing your site on the Internet. The simplest is to post a brief message describing your site (including its URL, of course) on relevant newsgroups (see Chapter 4) and listservs (see Chapter 2).

Next, you may want to try to get your site indexed on the major Web search engines and indexes. Most search engines have an "Add URL" feature that allows you to type your site's URL and a brief description that will appear when your site is listed in someone's search. In addition, you should specify the keywords you'd like your site to be listed under in your page's actual HTML file. You do this using the <META> tag, which goes in the <HEAD> section of your file. For example, the Trustbusters page might utilize Meta tags like this:

```
<HEAD>
<TITLE>A Century of Trustbusting</TITLE>
<META KEYWORDS="Antitrust, Microsoft, Bill
Gates, Standard Oil, John D. Rockefeller,
trustbusters, Sherman Anti-Trust Act, Social
Attitudes">
<META DESCRIPTION="An analysis of the effect of
and attitudes toward trustbusting and the
Microsoft Antitrust case">
</HEAD>
```

Publicizing Web sites has become an industry in itself. There are many sites devoted to Web site promotion, but the best is probably Jim Rhodes's The Art of Web Site Promotion at *http://www.deadlock.com/promote/*.

Advanced HTML techniques

Imagemaps and graphical links

One way to maximize the organizational potential of a Web site is to incorporate the use of imagemaps into its layout. An imagemap is a graphic image that has been "mapped" by HTML commands so that clicking on different portions of it will link the user to different sites or files, most often to different areas of a Web site. The author configures hot spots on the image, and a reader who clicks on one of the hot spots will be sent to whatever link has been assigned to that spot.

Imagemaps can be useful, as they provide a visual navigational tool for the site. We should caution that not all servers support imagemaps, and configuring the hot spots and links is somewhat sophisticated. Check with your server administrator before deciding to use imagemaps (for more information about making imagemaps, see *http://www.webcom.com /html/tutor/imagemaps.shtml*).

You do not need to use an imagemap to add graphical links to your Web site. By placing an image in a Web page and then creating a link from that image, you can design a site that uses visual elements to facilitate a reader's movement without having to learn the complex operation of imagemaps. Use small images to make links, and make sure the images convey a sense of the link to be followed; a small picture of a house, for example, could be used to indicate a return link to your home page.

Using forms to interact with a Web audience

A **form** is a mechanism by which Web browsers allow users to send information back to the server. If at all possible, include a comment form with each of your Web projects. Most comment forms are configured to send e-mail to the author of a Web page. Here is a sample comment form.

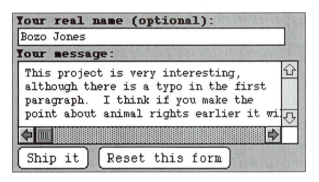

By using interactive comment forms, you can engage the Web's global audience. As with imagemaps, the ability to use interactive forms will depend upon the capacities of your Web server. Check with your server administrator about using forms. Many browsers now support the <MAILTO> HTML command, which can be configured to send e-mail to an author. If your server does not support forms, you should consider including a <MAILTO> option in your pages to facilitate contact. While the sample above shows the most basic contact form, you can modify forms to include fields for other information. (For more on forms, see *http://www.yahoo.com/Computers_and_Internet/Internet/World_Wide_Web/Programming/Forms/*).

A guide to HTML commands

Headings

```
<H1> . . . </H1>  largest heading
<H2> . . . </H2>
```

```
<H3> . . . </H2>
<H4> . . . </H4>
<H5> . . . </H5>
<H6> . . . </H6>  smallest heading
```

Font styles

`<B> . . . </B>`	**Bold-face text**
`<I> . . . </I>`	*Italicized text*
`<U> . . . </U>`	<u>Underlined text</u>
`<TT> . . . </TT>`	`Typewriter font`
`<STRIKE> . . . </STRIKE>`	~~Strike-through text~~
`<SUP> . . . </SUP>`	Superscript text
`<SUB> . . . </SUB>`	Subscript text
`<BIG> . . . </BIG>`	Large font
`<SMALL> . . . </SMALL>`	Small font
`<CENTER> . . . </CENTER>`	Centered material

Lists and menus

Definition list

```
<DL>
<DT>E-mail
<DD>The basic form
   of Internet com-
   munication.
<DT>Emote
<DD>Virtually rep-
   resents an ac-
   tion during
   real-time con-
   versations on
   IRCs and MOOs.
</DL>
```

E-mail
   The basic form of Internet communication.
Emote
   Virtually represents an action during real-time conversations on IRCs and MOOs.

Unnumbered list

```
<UL>
<LI>Milk
<LI>Bread
</UL>
```

- Milk
- Bread

Numbered list

```
<OL>
<LI>Milk
<LI>Bread
</OL>
```

1. Milk
2. Bread

Menu Lists

```
Heading
<MENU>
<LI>Milk
<LI>Bread
</MENU>
```

Heading
Milk
Bread

Links

The most common is the link to a document or file:

```
<A HREF="URL/file name"> . . . </A>
```

You can also make a link to a target within a document. Begin by placing a target anchor in the desired spot in the document.

```
<A NAME="target name">
```

Next make a link to the target by using the # sign and specifying the target name in the link information

```
<A HREF="#target name"> . . . </A>
```

You can also link to a sound, graphic, or video file by specifying the proper file name in the link information

	Links to:
`<A HREF="URL/filename.gif">...</A>`	gif image
`<A HREF="URL/filename.jpg">...</A>`	jpeg image
`<A HREF="URL/filename.mpg">...</A>`	mpeg movie
`<A HREF="URL/filename.mov">...</A>`	Quicktime movie
`<A HREF="URL/filename.au">...</A>`	sound file
`<A HREF ="URL/filename.wav">...</A>`	sound file

Inline Images

Inline images are graphics which are incorporated into the layout of a Web page. To place an inline image in a document, select the point in the document where the image should appear and use the command

```
<IMG ALIGN=bottom SRC="imagefilename.gif">
<IMG ALIGN=middle SRC="imagefilename.gif">
```

```
<IMG ALIGN=top SRC="imagefilename.gif">
<IMG ALIGN=left SRC="imagefilename.gif">
<IMG ALIGN=right SRC="imagefilename.gif">
```

Background Feature

The background attribute allows the user to specify an image file to use as a background for the Web page. This attribute is applied to the body element, discussed above. For example, at the beginning of the body section of a Web page, the element `<BODY BACKGROUND="imagename.gif">` tiles the window background with the designated GIF image. When the background attribute is utilized, the end tag to the body section is still simply: `</BODY>`.

Colors

Recently, the use of color on Web pages has expanded widely and is supported by most Web browsers. Colors can be given to a number of page elements. You can specify the most basic colors: `"White"`, `"Red"`, `"Green"`, etc. by just typing their names. In HTML, strict colors are designated by six-character codes representing their relative red/green/blue (RGB) values. Because of the complexity of these codes, you may want to use an HTML editor which supports the application of color. In such an editor, a shade is selected from a color wheel and the corresponding RGB values are placed automatically in the HTML script.

Also, you might refer to one of the many Web sites that provides the codes for the 216 shades that display correctly on both Macintosh and Windows platforms. (for example, *http://www.lightsphere.com/colors/*).

Colors are specified by using a hexadecimal value for each component of the color: red, green, blue. Two digits are allowed for each component, specified in the order red, green, blue. The lowest possible value for a color is 00; the highest value is FF. Hence, solid red would be FF0000, solid green would be 00FF00, solid black would be 000000, and solid white would be FFFFFF. You can specify millions of colors using these codes, but it is recommended you select from the 216 standard colors.

Colors are usually applied as attributes to the `<BODY>` element, and should be specified in the opening tag. If one of the following attributes is used, they should all be specified in order to avoid color conflicts. If, for example, a visitor to your page has set the Web browser to display text in the same color you gave to your background, this would make the page unreadable.

```
<BODY BGCOLOR="#rrggbb">        sets the background color
                                 for the page as a whole
<BODY TEXT="#rrggbb">           sets the text color for the
                                 page as a whole
<BODY LINK="#rrggbb">           sets the unvisited link
                                 color for the page as a
                                 whole
<BODY VLINK="#rrggbb">          sets the visited link color
                                 for the page as a whole
<BODY ALINK="#rrggbb">          sets the activated link
                                 color for the page as a
                                 whole
```

All these attributes should be specified in a single <BODY> tag, like so:

```
<BODY BGCOLOR="#FFFFFF" TEXT="#000000"
LINK="#FF0000" VLINK="#00FF00" ALINK="#00FF00">
```

Colors may also be applied to selected text within the body of a Web page. The element <FONT COLOR="#rrggbb"> . . . </FONT> will set the color of the text between the tags to the designated shade.

Tables

HTML tables are contained within <TABLE> . . . </TABLE> tags. The fundamental elements of an HTML table are <CAPTION>, which defines a caption for the table, and <TR>, which defines a table row. Each row in turn contains cells, either for a header, defined by <TH>, or for data, defined by <TD>. (Although in this example we are using only numerical data, text and even graphic files can be entered in a data cell as well.) Each cell should be closed with the appropriate ending tag, either </TH> or </TD>.

The caption may be aligned to the top, bottom, left, or right of the table by adding an ALIGN attribute to the <CAPTION> tag. By default, a table is flush with the left margin, but it can be centered by placing the entire table script within <CENTER> . . . </CENTER> tags. Additionally, a BORDER attribute may be added to the <TABLE> tag, which indicates that the table should be drawn with a border around it and between each of the table's cells. Adding a value (in number of pixels) sets the outer border of the table to the specified width.

To combine all these features, you can create a table using the following script:

```
<TABLE>
<CAPTION ALIGN="bottom">Academy Award Winning
African American Actors</Caption>
<TR><TH>Actor</TH><TH>Movie</TH>
<TH>Year</TH></TR>
<TR><TD>Whoopi Goldberg</TD><TD><I>Ghost</I>
</TD><TD>1991</TD></TR>
<TR><TD>Cuba Gooding Jr.</TD><TD><I>Jerry
Maguire</I></TD><TD>1997</TD></TR>
<TR><TD>Louis Gosset Jr.</TD><TD><I>An Officer
and a Gentleman</I></TD><TD>1983</TD></TR>
<TR><TD>Hattie McDaniel</TD><TD><I>Gone with the
Wind</I></TD><TD>1940</TD></TR>
<TR><TD>Sidney Poitier</TD><TD><I>Lilies of the
Field</I></TD><TD>1964</TD></TR>
<TR><TD>Denzel Washington</TD><TD><I>Glory</I>
</TD><TD>1990</TD></TR>
</TABLE>
```

The resulting table would be displayed as:

Actor	Movie	Year
Whoopi Goldberg	*Ghost*	1991
Cuba Gooding Jr.	*Jerry Maguire*	1997
Louis Gosset Jr.	*An Officer and a Gentleman*	1983
Hattie McDaniel	*Gone with the Wind*	1940
Sidney Poitier	*Lilies of the Field*	1964
Denzel Washington	*Glory*	1990
Academy Award Winning African American Actors		

You can also experiment with adding the CELLPADDING= and CELLSPACING= attributes to the <TABLE> element, which dictate (in number of pixels) the amount of space surrounding the contents of cells, and the width of the borders between cells, respectively. More complex tables are clearly illustrated on the Netscape Web site, at *http://home.netscape*

.com/assist/net_sites/tables.html. With their more advanced features, HTML tables can provide not simply a way to present data clearly, but a strategy for Web page design itself.

We can take our simple table above to the next level by specifying text more detailed and specific commands. Note that this level of precision requires much more code for what some would consider to be only an incremental improvement.

```
<BODY BGCOLOR="WHITE">
<TABLE CELLPADDING="0" CELLSPACING="0"
WIDTH="350">
<CAPTION ALIGN="bottom" WIDTH="350"><FONT
COLOR="Blue">Academy Award Winning African
American Actors</FONT></CAPTION>
<TR>
   <TD COLSPAN="3" WIDTH="350"><HR></TD>
</TR>
<TR>
   <TD HEIGHT="16" WIDTH="125"
   ALIGN="Left"><FONT
   COLOR="Red"><B>Actor</B></FONT></TD>
   <TD HEIGHT="16" WIDTH="175"
   ALIGN="Left"><FONT
   COLOR="Red"><B>Movie</B></FONT></TD>
   <TD HEIGHT="16" WIDTH="50" ALIGN="Left"><FONT
   COLOR="Red"><B>Year</B></FONT></TD>
</TR>
<TR>
   <TD COLSPAN="3" WIDTH="350"><HR></TD>
</TR>
<TR>
   <TD HEIGHT="16" WIDTH="125"
   ALIGN="Left">Whoopi Goldberg</TD>
   <TD HEIGHT="16" WIDTH="175"
   ALIGN="Left"><I>Ghost</I></TD>
   <TD HEIGHT="16" WIDTH="50"
   ALIGN="Left">1991</TD>
</TR>
<TR>
   <TD HEIGHT="16" WIDTH="125" ALIGN="Left">Cuba
   Gooding Jr.</TD>
   <TD HEIGHT="16" WIDTH="175"
   ALIGN="Left"><I>Jerry Maguire</I></TD>
   <TD HEIGHT="16" WIDTH="50"
   ALIGN="Left">1997</TD>
</TR>
<TR>
   <TD HEIGHT="16"  WIDTH="125"
```

```
   ALIGN="Left">Louis Gosset Jr.</TD>
   <TD HEIGHT="16" WIDTH="175"
   ALIGN="Left"><I>An Officer and a
   Gentleman</I></TD>
   <TD HEIGHT="16" WIDTH="50"
   ALIGN="Left">1983</TD>
</TR>
<TR>
   <TD HEIGHT="16" WIDTH="125"
   ALIGN="Left">Hattie McDaniel</TD>
   <TD HEIGHT="16" WIDTH="175"
   ALIGN="Left"><I>Gone with the Wind</I></TD>
   <TD HEIGHT="16" WIDTH="50"
   ALIGN="Left">1940</TD>
</TR>
<TR>
   <TD HEIGHT="16" WIDTH="125"
   ALIGN="Left">Sidney Poitier</TD>
   <TD HEIGHT="16" WIDTH="175"
   ALIGN="Left"><I>Lilies of the Field</I></TD>
   <TD HEIGHT="16" WIDTH="50"
   ALIGN="Left">1964</TD>
</TR>
<TR>
   <TD HEIGHT="16" WIDTH="125"
   ALIGN="Left">Denzel Washington</TD><TD
   HEIGHT="16" WIDTH="175"
   ALIGN="Left"><I>Glory</I></TD>
   <TD HEIGHT="16" WIDTH="50"
   ALIGN="Left">1990</TD>
</TR>
<TR>
   <TD COLSPAN="3" WIDTH="350"><HR></TD>
</TR>
</TABLE>
</BODY>
```

This code produces the following table:

Actor	Movie	Year
Whoopi Goldberg	*Ghost*	1991
Cuba Gooding Jr.	*Jerry Maguire*	1997
Louis Gosset Jr.	*An Officer and a Gentleman*	1983
Hattie McDaniel	*Gone with the Wind*	1940
Sidney Poitier	*Lilies of the Field*	1964
Denzel Washington	*Glory*	1990

Academy Award Winning African American Actors

Note that the specification of a width and height for each table cell allows precise control over the positioning of each element in the table. We used the COLSPAN attribute to generate horizontal rules extending all the way across the table.

You can use tables to position graphics and text as precisely as if you were laying them out on paper. When you're using tables and other high-level tricks to give your page a particular look, make sure you test them on both Netscape and Microsoft browsers, to verify that all visitors to your site have the same experience.

If you're interested in using tables to give very fine control of the look of your entire Web site, visit David Siegel's Creating Killer Web Sites at *http://www.killersites.com/tutorial/index.html.*

Becoming an HTML expert

Believe it or not, most HTML experts didn't get that way by reading a lot of books about it. Books have their place, but the best way to learn the tricks of the trade is to see how others have done the kinds of things you'd like to do. Because HTML documents are designed to be viewed on a variety of platforms, their source HTML code is available to anyone who knows where to look. The best HTML programmers learned their trade by looking what others have done and then combining that knowledge with their own creative energy.

When you're visiting any Web page, you can look at the source code for that page simply by selecting the View source command from the File menu. The raw HTML for that page will appear—usually in a helper application.

If you look carefully at the HTML tags for the page, you'll soon learn how the designer created the page. You can use the same strategy in your own HTML code. Take care, however, when you use someone else's ideas. Learning how to use HTML by looking at someone else's source code is all right, but copying someone's words, images, or design can be a violation of copyright laws. See the Appendix for a discussion of copyright law and the Internet.

For more information about HTML commands, visit the Introduction to HTML and URLs site at *http://www.utoronto.ca/webdocs/HTMLdocs/NewHTML/intro.html.*

Chapter 8

Documenting Electronic Sources

Major documentation systems like the APA and the MLA have recently incorporated guidelines for citing Internet sources in their style guides; however, we think their suggestions fail to provide the necessary citation information for Internet resources because they duplicate the format of traditional documentation forms without accommodating the particular demands of the Internet.

The *MLA Handbook* offers the following guide for Internet sources:

Material accessed through a computer network
1. Name of author (if given)
2. Title of article or document (in quotation marks)
3. Title of the journal, newsletter, or conference (underlined)
4. Volume number, issue number or other identifying number
5. Year of date of publication (in parentheses)
6. Number of pages or paragraphs (if given) or n.pag ("no pagination")
7. Publication medium (online)
8. Name of computer network
9. Date of access

A sample entry would look like this:

```
Moulthrop, Stuart. "You Say You Want a
    Revolution? Hypertext and the Laws of
```

```
Media." Postmodern Culture 1. (1991): 53
pars. Online BITNET. 10 Jan. 1993
```

According to the MLA, at the end of the entry you may add as supplementary information the electronic address you used to access the document; precede the address with the word "Available." They note that "[y]our instructor may require this information."

Though it is a convention that tries to indicate the existence of Internet sources, this system does little to handle the unique nature of Internet publications. Simply telling a reader that a source can be found "online" does little to help a researcher find the source document. It would be very difficult to locate this source again and to determine if you had the same version of the document. Because of the Internet's vast scope and changing nature, it is especially important to provide the exact path by which you found a document and to distinguish between the date you found the source and its publication date (if it has one).

ACW documentation

Janice R. Walker of the University of South Florida has developed a style guide for handling Internet resources that distinguishes between different protocols and highlights the importance of addresses in each. The components of her reference citation are simply:

```
Author's Last Name, First Name. "Title of
Work." Title of Complete Work. [protocol
and address] [path] (date of message or
visit).
```

In addition, Walker has placed a style sheet on the World Wide Web that provides a documentation system for all the Internet media we cover in this book. A copy of this style sheet follows. We would recommend using this style sheet as an addition to the MLA handbook in order to cite Internet sources.

Internet style sheet
http://www.cas.usf.edu/english/walker/mla.html
(Endorsed by the Alliance for Computers and Writing)

FTP (File Transfer Protocol) Sites

To cite files available for downloading via FTP, give the author's name (if known), the full title of the paper in quo-

tation marks, and the address of the FTP site along with the
full path to follow to find the paper, and the date of access.

```
Bruckman, Amy. "Approaches to Managing
    Deviant Behavior in Virtual Communities."
    ftp.media.mit.edu pub/asb/papers/deviance-
    chi94 (4 Dec.1994).
```

WWW Sites (World Wide Web)
(Available via Lynx, Netscape, other Web Browsers)
To cite files available for viewing/downloading via the
World Wide Web, give the author's name (if known), the full
title of the work in quotation marks, the title of the complete
work (if applicable) in italics, the full *http* address, and the
date of visit.

```
Burka, Lauren P. "A Hypertext History of
    Multi-User Dimensions." MUD History.
    http://www.ccs.neu.edu/home/lpb/mud-his-
    tory.html (5 Dec. 1994).
```

Telnet Sites
(Sites and files available via the Telnet protocol)
List the author's name (if known), the title of the work (if
shown) in quotation marks, the title of the full work (if applicable) in italics, and the complete Telnet address, along
with directions to access the publication, along with the date
of visit.

```
Gomes, Lee. "Xerox's On-Line Neighborhood: A
    Great Place to Visit." Mercury News 3 May
    1992. Telnet lambda.parc.xerox.com 8888,
    @go #50827, press 13 (5 Dec. 1994).
```

Synchronous Communications
(MOOs, MUDs, IRC, etc.)
Give the name of the speaker(s) and type of communication (i.e., Personal Interview), the address (if applicable) and
the date in parentheses.

```
Pine_Guest. Personal Interview. Telnet
    world.sensemedia.net 1234 (12 Dec. 1994).
WorldMOO Christmas Party. Telnet
    world.sensemedia.net 1234 (24 Dec. 1994).
```

Gopher Sites
(Information available via Gopher search protocols)

For information found using Gopher search protocols, list the author's name, the title of the paper in quotation marks, any print publication information, and the Gopher search path followed to access the information, including the date that the file was accessed.

```
Quittner, Joshua. "Far Out: Welcome to Their
    World Built·of MUD." Published in
    Newsday, 7 Nov. 1993. Gopher /University
    of Koeln/About MUDs, MOOs and MUSEs in
    Education/Selected Papers/newsday (5 Dec.
    1994).
```

E-mail, listserv, and newslist citations

Give the author's name (if known), the subject line from the posting in quotation marks, and the address of the listserv or newslist, along with the date. For personal e-mail listings, the address may be omitted.

```
Bruckman, Amy S. "MOOSE Crossing Proposal."
    mediamoo@media.mit.edu (20 Dec. 1994).
Seabrook, Richard H. C. "Community and
    Progress." cybermind@jefferson.village
    .virginia.edu (22 Jan. 1994).
Thomson, Barry. "Virtual Reality." Personal
    e-mail (25 Jan. 1995).
```

Chapter 9

Researching Literature on the Internet

Researching literature on the Internet poses some unique challenges. Writing has traditionally required only a pen or pencil and paper, and it has taken a while for the literary community to catch up with the high-tech world. Also, because the literary community is often painfully aware of the complexities of copyright law, it has shown some reluctance to place literary works and works of criticism on the Internet. And because "publishing" has always been the primary goal for "serious" poets, dramatists, writers, and critics, the Internet may have suffered, because publishing a work there isn't generally considered to be the same as "real" publishing.

With those concerns in mind, the Internet can provide tremendous resources for literature researchers. These resources tend to be the most comprehensive in two areas— works like Shakespeare's plays or the poems of Elizabeth Barret Browning whose copyrights have expired, and "non-traditional" literature such as cowboy poetry which has often been excluded from the mainstream press. There is also a considerable amount of biographical information on individual authors. Popular authors like Kurt Vonnegut may even have several fan pages. Newsgroups and listservs offer up-to-the-minute conversations on current issues in literature and criticism. Finally, the Internet has made the libraries of the world accessible to everyone—provided you allow enough time to request their materials via interlibrary loan.

Authors on the Web

Before you start writing about your topic, it always helps to get some information about the author. If you've decided to write on *Hamlet,* for example, you can start by looking up information on Shakespeare. Since Shakespeare is by most accounts the central figure of English literature, it is easy to find information about his life on the Internet. There are bibliographic Web pages, as well as a newsgroup devoted to him. You can even find discussions and Web pages arguing whether or not Shakespeare existed.

The Web is also a good tool to use if you are studying an author who is still alive. Many authors have their own Web pages, and almost all have e-mail. Unlike popular novelists and screenwriters, contemporary poets aren't typically deluged with fan mail. Depending on how busy they are—and how carefully crafted your messages are—you may be able to engage a poet in an electronic discussion of her work. The links below should help you get started.

The Shakespeare Mystery
http://www2.pbs.org/wgbh/pages/frontline/shakespeare/

The Author Guru's List of Author Addresses
http://www.geocities.com/Athens/Acropolis/4617/author mail.html

Playwrights on the Web
http://ourworld.compuserve.com/homepages/paul_thain /playwrig.htm

An Index of Poets in Representative Poetry On-line
http://library.utoronto.ca/www/utel/rp/indexauthors.html

The Academy of American Poets
http://www.poets.org/

Newsgroups and listservs

Once you've found some general information about the author you're studying, you may want to begin a discussion with others on the Internet. Newsgroups and listservs allow you to see what others have to say about your topic in an informal setting. You can use them to bounce ideas off others interested in the same issues you have, and to see what others have already said.

When you're brainstorming for a topic, looking through the past postings might give you an idea for your paper just by seeing what other people are talking about. For example, the Shakespeare newsgroup (*humanities.lit.authors.shakespeare*) has discussed such topics as which *Hamlet* movie is the best, the true authorship of Shakespeare's plays, and even some humorous inferences based on Shakespeare's works.

Once you have an idea for a topic you can post your own message to get feedback about your ideas. Remember, when posting to listservs and newsgroups, take care to compose a posting that shows you've put some serious thought into the topic. The message: "I am writing a paper on *Hamlet*, can anyone help me?" will probably only get sarcastic responses if it gets any responses at all. A carefully composed request that perks the interest of others in the group is much more likely to generate useful and interesting responses. For example, you might say, "I am writing a paper on madness in *Hamlet* and believe the changes that take place in Ophelia's character are symptomatic of manic depression. Are there any Internet or printed resources that might help confirm this hypothesis?" Now instead of simply asking for help, you've opened up an interesting issue for debate among group members—and you'll probably get help on your paper in the process.

Remember when you post to a newsgroup or listserv that your readers are typically scanning through a long list of subject headings. Make sure you write a subject line that grabs your reader's attention, or your message will very likely be ignored. While group members will very likely pass by a subject line like "Hamlet Paper," they'd probably be intrigued by a heading like "Is Ophelia a Manic Depressive?"

Listservs are similar to newsgroups in their on-going dialogue between subscribers. But listservs also put you at the mercy of the group because the only discussion or feedback you receive comes to you through e-mail as it is posted. Unlike newsgroups, listservs often offer no way to browse past conversations or to look for a specific topic. However, most listservs offer a way to request an index of past messages and retrieve the messages you want. For information on how to do this, check out the **FAQ** file for your listserv.

When you use newsgroups and listservs for information, be aware that the person writing the message may not be an expert. Even if you do find the opinions of an expert, be aware that most newsgroup and listserv postings are fairly hastily and casually composed. If you find a well-formed opinion that you'd like to cite in your own research, make sure you give your source proper credit (see chapter 8), and save a copy of the posting.

Here are a few listservs and newsgroups you may want to check out. There are hundreds more available. For information on how to subscribe to a listserv, see pages 20–21.

http://www.liszt.com/
The Web's premier search engine for listservs and newsgroups.

Listservs
mesaverde
majordomo@lists.uoregon.edu
Discusses literary and ecological issues

AMLIT-L
listproc@listis.missouri.edu
A large listserv discussing American Literature

Newsgroups
Beat Generation
alt.books.beatgeneration

Shakespeare
humanities.lit.authors.shakespeare

General literature discussion
tnn.literature

Text of works on the Web

While most copyrighted books and journals are not freely available on the Web, famous works whose copyrights have expired can be found in abundance. In the United States, all copyrights for works published more than seventy-five years ago have expired, so if you're writing about a work over seventy-five years old, you may very likely find the complete text on the Web. In Great Britain, copyrights expire fifty years after the death of the author, so you may even find some works less than seventy-five years old on the Web (for example, many works of D. H. Lawrence can be found at the Bibliomania Web site, *http://www.bibliomania.com/Fiction/dhl/*).

So what good is the text on the Internet if you already have a printed copy? Let's suppose, after browsing through

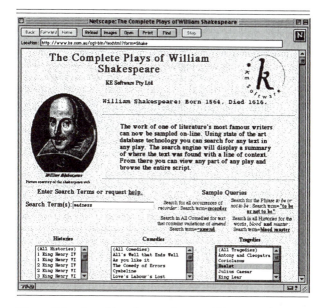

Figure 9.1:   Searching for *madness* on The Complete
Plays of William Shakespeare site

some newsgroups, you have decided to write on madness in
Hamlet. The complete works of Shakespeare are readily
available on the Web, and some are even searchable. For example, you could search *Hamlet* on The Complete Plays of
William Shakespeare at *http://www.ke.com.au/cgi-bin/
texhtml?form=Shake*. A search for *madness* finds twenty-two
instances of this word. You can click on the word in the sample to be sent to the scene where the word was found.

It is important to look for alternate spellings or synonyms
as well. *Mad* returned twenty-one instances, *sick* had four,
and there were none for *crazy* and *dementia*. If the work you
are using does not have its own searchable database, you can
conduct your own search of the text by using the "Find"
command of your browser.

While counting instances of key words does not substitute for a close analysis of the text itself, searching Web text
can alert you to key passages you may not have noticed otherwise. Some Web search engines even allow commands like
"before" and "close to" which can further limit your search.
Below are several sites which offer searchable text of literary
works.

IPL Online Texts Collection
http://www.ipl.org/reading/books/

Electronic Text Center—University of Virginia
http://etext.lib.virginia.edu/english.html

The On-Line Books Page
http://www.cs.cmu.edu/books.html

Selected Poetry of Robert Browning (1812–1889)
*http://library.utoronto.ca/www/utel/rp/authors/browning
.html*

The Internet Classics Archive
http://classics.mit.edu/

Geoffrey Chaucer (ca.1343–1400)
http://www.luminarium.org/medlit/chaucer.htm

GEOFFREY CHAUCER ca. 1343–1400
*http://federalist.com/poetry/GEOFFREYCHAUCERcahall
/wwwboard.html*

IPL William Shakespeare's Complete Works
http://www.ipl.org/reading/shakespeare/shakespeare.html

Edmund Spenser Home Page
http://darkwing.uoregon.edu/~rbear/

Isle of Lesbos: Lesbian Poetry
http://www.sappho.com/poetry/

The Academy of American Poets
http://www.poets.org/

Criticism on the Web

As the Internet becomes more accessible, critical works are becoming more readily available on the Web. There are many online journals and print journals that publish articles on the Web. However, the Internet's resources are still insubstantial compared to what's available in printed journals. For example, Oxford University Press publishes over 180 journals, but none of them are available free of charge on the Web. A few resources are available, and some may even provide information you can't find anywhere else, but with literary criticism in particular, the vast majority of what's out there is still only available in print.

When you do find critical resouces on the Web, make sure you evaluate the reliability of the source. In academic journals, you should be able to find the submission requirements, which will tell you how the editors determine what is published. The most important publication standard for academic journals is peer review. If you know that a journal article has been reviewed by a critic's academic colleagues, you have good evidence that your source is reliable. This is not to say that there won't be disagreement in the academic community with the opinions presented in the article, but peer review gives you some assurance that an article represents a valid, well-thought perspective on a topic.

If an article has not been subjected to peer review, it doesn't necessarily mean the opinion presented is wrong. It may, however, mean the opinion is not a mainstream one. In cases such as this, use the guidelines on pages 5–6 to assess the reliability of the document. For example, one *Hamlet* page full of notes and essays, *http://www.vaxxine.com/megs/hamlet.html*, was created by a sixteen-year-old and contains notes from her high school English class. Although the information here may be reliable, it would probably be best to confirm it using another source.

Criticism links
Elizabethan Review
http://www.elizreview.com/

The Hamlet Home Page
http://www.hamlet.edmonton.ab.ca/

Ophelia
http://www.stg.brown.edu/projects/hypertext/landow/victorian/gender/ophelia.html

Sewanee Review
http://cloud9.sewanee.edu/sreview/Home.html

Hypermedia Joyce Studies
http://astro.temple.edu/~callahan/hjs/hjs.html

MFS
http://www.sla.purdue.edu/academic/engl/mfs/#ABOUT

Individual critics' sites

You can also use the Internet as a source for information on famous theorists, including some of their works, short biographies, and other writings about their works. Again, it is important to check the reliability of the sources on many of these writings.

Bakhtin on-line elsewhere
http://hippo.shef.ac.uk/uni/academic/A-C/bakh/online.html

Postmodernism, deconstructionism, criticism, and literary theory campfire messsage board
http://killdevilhill.com/postmodernchat/wwwboard.html

An Introduction to Literary Criticism—Contents
http://www.more.net/~mike/critcont.html

Literary and Critical Theory
http://www.stg.brown.edu/projects/hypertext/landow/SSPCluster/theorists.html

Voice of the Shuttle: Literary Theory Page
http://humanitas.ucsb.edu/shuttle/theory.html

Using the Internet to find off-line sources

Once you have exhausted the supply of information on the Internet, you can still use it to search the on-line catalogs of other libraries for books. Most online library catalogs are similar to each other, but it is helpful to read the search directions for each one to ensure that you are getting the best responses. You can also search indexes, such as Carl UnCover. This particular index provides access to journal articles, which they can fax to you for a fee.

Library of Congress WWW/Z39.50 Gateway
http://lcweb.loc.gov/z3950/gateway.html#other

Other interesting literature sites

There are literally thousands of literature sites on the Web. The following listing comprises just a few of the more interesting/unique ones.

Poetry Daily, a new poem every day
http://www.poems.com/~poems/home.htm

LitLinks
http://www.ualberta.ca/~amactavi/litlinks.htm

Zuzu's Petals Literary Links: General Reference Tools
http://www.lehigh.net/zuzu/genlink.htm

VoS English Literature: English Literature Page
http://humanitas.ucsb.edu/shuttle/english.html

The English Server
http://english.hss.cmu.edu/

Tree fiction on the World Wide Web
http://www.cl.cam.ac.uk/users/gdr11/tree-fiction.html
#Feedback

Appendix

Copyright Issues

Students and instructors increasingly have to work with copyright considerations as they prepare their course material. The "fair use clause" of the U.S. Copyright Act gives instructors and student researchers some flexibility when it comes to using copyrighted materials in class:

> Not withstanding the provisions of sections 106 and 106A [17 USCS §§ 106, 106A] the fair use of a copyrighted work, including such use by reproduction in copies or phonorecords or by any other means specified by that section, for purposes such as criticism, comment, news reporting, teaching (including multiple copies for classroom use), scholarship, or research, is not an infringement of copyright. In determining whether the use made of a work in any particular case is a fair use the factors to be considered shall include—
>
> 1. the purpose and character of the use, including whether such use is of a commercial nature or is for nonprofit educational purposes;
> 2. the nature of the copyrighted work;
> 3. the amount and substantiality of the portion used in relation to the copyrighted work as a whole; and
> 4. the effect of the use upon the potential market for or value of the copyrighted work.
>
> The fact that a work is unpublished shall not itself bar a finding of fair use if such finding is made upon consideration of all the above factors.

Under these guidelines, it is possible to make use of copyrighted materials for the purpose of instruction and coursework. However, the inter-connectedness and spontaneous nature of the Internet complicates the notion of what constitutes the fair use of copyrighted materials. For example, duplicating an essay or an ad from a magazine for use in class might fall under the guidelines for fair use of copyrighted material because it is done for scholarly or critical purposes and not intended to make a profit. Posting the same material to a class newsgroup, however, might not be acceptable because it would be available to an audience outside the classroom and this availability might diminish the value of the original document. Perhaps even sending the article as an e-mail message would have the same effect, since e-mail messages are often forwarded to secondary parties. Posting materials on the World Wide Web compounds the problem of fair use because most Web browsers allow users to download any materials they find and to incorporate the source documents of Web pages into their own sites.

Because of the simplicity of distributing materials on the Internet, making clear distinctions about the boundaries of copyrighted materials becomes difficult. The rights of intellectual property owners should be balanced with those of individuals who wish to participate in the free exchange of ideas. In their statement, "Fair Use in the Electronic Age: Serving the Public Interest" the American Library Association suggests that the balance between the owner's claims to intellectual property and the public's interest in the free exchange of ideas should be honored in electronic space.

> The primary objective of copyright is not to reward the labor of authors, but "[t]o promote the Progress of Science and useful Arts." To this end, copyright assures authors the right to their original expression, but encourages others to build freely upon the ideas and information conveyed by a work. . . . This result is neither unfair nor unfortunate. It is the means by which copyright advances the progress of science and art. —Justice Sandra Day O'Connor (*Feist Publications, Inc. v. Rural Telephone Service Co.,* 499 US 340, 349 [1991]). The genius of United States copyright law is that, in conformance with its constitutional foundation, it balances the intellectual property interests of authors, publishers and copyright owners with society's need for the free exchange of ideas.

The guidelines of the fair use clause can be applied to the Internet as well, but many of the issues relating to electronic use of material and particularly electronic scholarly use, are still unresolved. Some guidelines include using no more materials than necessary to make a given point or to develop an idea and considering whether using materials will devalue them in any way for the owner.

You will also find some material already online which probably shouldn't be, for example scanned pictures, unauthorized reproductions of texts, film clips, and sound files. When evaluating sources, consider the implications of using materials which are available online but which may not be in the public domain, and strive to comply with fair use guidelines. Likewise, there are no mechanisms in place on the Internet for assuring that the material you post online won't at some point be downloaded and made use of in less-than-responsible ways.

Glossary

@ (the "at" sign) Used to separate the mailbox name from the domain name in e-mail addresses.

absolute URL The complete URL; used to refer to URLs outside of the current domain.

address Specialized URL for sending e-mail, consisting of a mailbox name and the domain name, separated by the @ sign. Also used to refer to any URL.

anchor The beginning point for a hypertext link. Anchors usually use underlined text (hot text) or images to indicate links.

angle bracket (>) 1. Used to denote a reply quotation in e-mail messages. 2. Used in pairs to surround HTML tags.

application Any type of commercial, shareware, or freeware computer program (usually with a user interface).

Archie A protocol which allows keyword searches of the contents of FTP sites (primarily for names of freeware and shareware applications and graphic files).

ASCII text (Pron. *askey*) Also known as "text only" format, the basic, unformatted numbers, letters, and symbols supported by most computer operating systems.

asynchronous Communication or other interaction that takes place with a substantial delay, e.g., e-mail, answering machines.

attribute (HTML) A modification to an HTML tag which gives information about how it is to be applied.

117

AU An audio file format commonly found on the World Wide Web.

authoring The process of creating hypermedia content for the World Wide Web.

bit The smallest unit of computer memory. Can have only two values, 1 or 0.

bookmark An electronic pointer to a Gopher, FTP, or Web site that can be recalled for future reference. A list of bookmarks is known as a "hotlist."

Boolean Logical search operators that allow a user to refine the scope of keyword searches. The simple Boolean operators are *and, or,* and *not.*

bots (robots) Objects in MOO environments which are programmed to interact with readers.

browser A client which allows users to view pages on the World Wide Web. The two most popular browsers are Microsoft Internet Explorer and Netscape Navigator.

browsing The process of viewing Web pages with a browser.

byte A unit of computer memory corresponding to eight bits. A byte contains enough information to specify one character.

CD-ROM A compact disc used for storing computer files. Many new formats have been introduced recently, including CD-RW, DVD, and CD-R.

channel Also referred to as a "line." An IRC channel is roughly equivalent to a CB radio frequency. Users join a channel to participate in the discussion that takes place among people logged on to that frequency.

chat 1. A somewhat derogatory term used to describe newsgroups or listservs that are geared towards the discussion of nonacademic topics. 2. A term often heard when talking about Internet Relay Chat (IRC). The IRC channels are often called "chat lines" and the conversations that take place on these channels are often referred to as "chat."

Clarinet Newsfeeds from Reuters and the Associated Press in the form of Usenet newsgroups. Institutions must pay a fee in order to subscribe to groups provided by the Clarinet company.

client Software which communicates with a server to provide an easier interface for a user.

Common Gateway Interface (CGI) A program which resides on a server and handles complex information requests. CGIs act as mediators between a source of information on a server and a client. They are most commonly used to process forms in HTML.

compression Manipulation of a file to decrease the amount of memory it consumes. Compression can be either *lossy*, meaning some information is lost in compression, or *lossless*, meaning all information is retained.

directory A subdivision in a computer file system (known as a "folder" in some operating systems). Directories can contain files, applications, or other directories.

directory path The complete set of nested directories needed to locate a particular file. In URLs, each directory name is separated by a slash.

discussion list See *listserv.*

domain An element of an Internet or e-mail address specified by an organization or sub-organization on the Internet (e.g., netscape.com, or utexas.edu).

DOS See *operating system.*

downloading Retrieving a file or application from a remote host over the Internet.

element (HTML) Instructions within an HTML document, along with the text to which they apply. For example, the boldface text element, `<B> this text will be bold </B>`.

e-mail (electronic mail) A form of Internet communication used to send all types of electronic correspondence to individuals or groups of Internet-connected users around the world.

e-mail address See *address.*

emote To virtually represent an action during the real-time conversations on IRCs and MOOs. For example, a user named Socrates could type `:listens intently`, and the text transmitted to other participants would read `Socrates listens intently`.

emoticons Pictures made of text symbols attempting to express emotions in e-mail messages, newsgroup postings, and real-time discussions. The basic Internet emoticon is the "smiley," a sideways happy face: :-) (Turn your head to the left to see it).

FAQ (Frequently Asked Questions) A document which collects and responds to some of the most common questions about a particular aspect of the Internet or about a particular topic, especially newsgroups and listservs.

favorites See *bookmark*.

file An electronic document. Files can be in ASCII text, in a format for a particular program, or in a standardized format for sound, graphics, or video (e.g., WAV, GIF, or MPEG).

file name The name of a file, including any extensions such as *.html* or *.gif*, but not including its directory path.

flame A message or posting attacking a message or an individual. A flame usually has a confrontational tone and offers little or no constructive criticism.

form (HTML) Mechanism which allows Web site visitors to send information back to a server.

freeware Software distributed free of charge.

FTP (File Transfer Protocol) An early, but still frequently used system of downloading and uploading files on the Internet.

fuzzy search A search for any occurence of a sequence of characters, regardless of whether they form an entire word.

GIF (Graphical Interchange Format) (pron. *jiff*) A compressed graphics file format frequently used for images on the World Wide Web. GIF files save memory by limiting the number of colors in an image.

Gopher A system of Internet protocols and directory structures that allows users to connect to remote hosts, access directories of information, and download files. In addition, Gopher sites can be searched for directory names, file titles, or text contained in individual files.

Gopher server A centralized server that offers hierarchically organized information to a user via a Gopher client. Also called Gopherhost.

Gopherspace   The realm of the Internet dedicated to Gopher. A good place to find archaic computer programming jokes.

hardware   The mechanical portion of a computer system.

hit   1. An item returned from a keyword search. 2. A single visit to a Web site.

home page   Conventional name given to a central site on the World Wide Web. This name can be used both for the central page of an organization site and for the personal page of an individual within an organization.

host   1. An Internet-connected machine which serves files to various clients. 2. Any Internet-connected machine.

hotlist   See *bookmark*.

hot text   Text in a hypertext document which is linked to another document. The most common way of linking documents on the Web. Hot text is generally colored and underlined to indicate that clicking on it will take the user to another document.

HTML (Hypertext Markup Language)   A scripting language used to turn plain text and other elements (such as images) into the integrated pages we see on the Web.

HTTP (Hypertext Transport Protocol)   An Internet protocol which allows for the transfer of hypertext files from a Web server to a Web client application.

hypermedia   A medium which extends the principles of hypertext to document types other than text.

hypertext   A text authoring medium with no predetermined organizational structure which allows authors to freely link any portion of a document with any other portion, or with other documents.

image editor   An application which allows users to create and edit image files.

imagemap   An image which has been "mapped" by HTML commands so that clicking on different portions of it will link the user to different sites or files.

inline image   An image which has been inserted into the design of a Web page.

interface   The features of an application which mediate a user's interaction with the program. Generally speaking, the more intuitive the interface is to a user, the easier it will be to run the program.

Internet The worldwide network of computers that allows distribution of e-mail, browsing the Web, and countless other ways to access and distribute information.

IP address (Internet Protocol Address) The address which is specific to a single computer and identifies it for the purpose of interacting with other computers on the Internet.

IRC (Internet Relay Chat) A system of Internet protocols and programs which allow users to participate on topic-centered, real-time discussion channels.

Java A programming language which allows computers running on different operating systems to run the same programs. Java functions, typically used for graphics, animation, or complex data management tasks, are actually performed by applications (*applets*) which reside on servers rather than individual PCs.

JPEG (from *Joint Photographic Experts Group*, pron. *JAY-peg*) A graphics file format frequently used for images on the World Wide Web. JPEG files are typically most effective for photographs and offer several different levels of compression, with higher compression resulting in more loss of file resolution.

kilobyte (K) A unit of computer memory corresponding to 1,024 bytes.

link A hypertext connection between documents, sites, and other media. Note that *link* is commonly used both as a noun to indicate the actual connection between one node and another, and as a verb to indicate the process by which this connection is achieved.

Listproc A type of mailing list software. See also *listserv*.

listserv Also known as a "mailing list" or "list." A program which allows mail to be sent to a group of addresses at once.

literal search A search for an exact phrase or grouping of words, usually indicated with quotation marks.

local In the same directory as the current file. In HTML coding, local files can be accessed using relative URLs.

lurk To read a newsgroup or e-mail list for a period of time without posting messages.

Macintosh See *operating system*. See also *platform*.

mailbox name The specific identification or name given to an e-mail user. In conjunction with the domain name, it makes up the e-mail address using the syntax `mailboxname@domainname`.

mailreader Also known as a "mail client." A program which provides an easy interface for reading, composing, posting, and downloading e-mail messages.

mail server A server which organizes, stores, and distributes e-mail messages to various users.

Majordomo A type of mailing list software. See also *listserv*.

modem Short for "modulater-demodulater," a device used to connect computers via a telephone line or other communication link to a server. When you connect to the Internet at school your workstation may be directly wired to a server, but if you connect at home you will most likely need to use a modem.

moderator Person responsible for determining the relevancy of messages posted to a moderated newsgroup or listserv. A moderator forwards only "appropriate" messages to the group.

MOV/MOOV A video format often used on the World Wide Web.

MPEG (pron. *empeg*) A video format often used on the World Wide Web.

MU*s (also MUSHs, Tiny MUSHs, MOOs, etc.) Text-based virtual spaces ("Multi User Dungeons" or "Domains") which allow users to interact in real time with other users or with the textual environment. The different acronyms refer to different programs which perform similar functions.

name search A search for the first and last name of a person. Usually indicated by capitalizing both terms.

netiquette A set of rules for behavior on the Internet, usually dictated by convenience and common sense.

newsfeed A message posted to a newsgroup which originates from a wire service or other traditional news source.

newsgroups Topic-centered sites where visitors can exchange articles, messages, or other media. See also *Usenet*.

newsreader A news client.

news server Also known as a news host. A server which organizes, stores, and distributes newsgroup messages.

nickname 1. An address book entry for one or more e-mail addresses. When a user types the nickname, the computer sends that message to each of the addresses in the nickname file. 2. A character name used to log on to IRC channels.

node A hypertextual site which organizes multiple links. Nodes can contain any combination of text, links, graphics, sound, and video.

operating system The software which controls the basic operations of the computer. Examples include MacOS, DOS, and Unix. These systems are generally incompatible with each other.

page Part of a Web site corresponding to a single HTML file.

PC 1. Also referred to as "IBM compatible," indicates a computer which runs the DOS operating system (usually with the graphical user interface Windows). 2. Used less often to indicate any personal computer.

Photo CD A type of CD-ROM containing photo images. Also used to refer to the format Photo CD images are saved in.

pixel A single dot, or element, of a picture. Image sizes on the Web are measured in pixels.

platform A computer with a given type of operating system, for example, Macintosh, PC, or Unix.

post 1. To send an electronic message to an e-mail discussion list or newsgroup. Also used as a noun to refer to the message itself. 2. To upload a Web site to a Web server.

protocol The "language" that a client and server use to distinguish various types of Internet media.

readme file Gives information about a piece of software or an Internet forum. Titling a file "readme" almost assures that it will never be read.

real time Communication or other interaction that occurs almost instantaneously, as in IRCs and MOOs, allowing users to communicate in a way which resembles face-to-face conversation. Contrast to e-mail and newsgroup messages, which are *asynchronous*.

relative URL A partial URL used to specify locations within the current domain.

reply quotation A copy of a message which is included in the reply to the message. Most mail clients and news-readers place angled brackets (>) in front of a quotation in order to distinguish it from a new message.

robot search engine A search engine which automatically visits Web sites or other Internet sites and catalogs them based on a predetermined set of criteria.

scanner A machine which converts photographs and other physical images into electronic files.

search engine A program usually accessed via a Web site that allows users to perform keyword searches on the Internet (e.g., AltaVista, Infoseek).

search index A directory of services on the Internet orga-nized hierarchically.

server 1. Software that provides information to client pro-grams. Clients and servers "talk" to each other to allow the transfer of files and protocols across the Internet. 2. The machine on which a server program is located.

shareware Like *freeware*, software which is made available through the Internet. The authors of shareware ask for a small voluntary fee from users.

shell A program that interprets commands typed at a ter-minal.

signature file Pre-formatted text attached to the bottom of most e-mail and newsgroup messages which generally con-tains the author's name, e-mail address, and institutional affiliation (if any). Signature files can also contain carefully constructed ASCII text pictures and favorite quotations.

site A collection of documents on the Internet providing a single set information to users who access the location.

slide show A series of textual screens that scroll by to deliver information in a MOO.

smiley See *emoticon*.

software A computer program written to perform various tasks, as opposed to *hardware* which refers to the mechanical parts of a computer system. See also *application.*

source document The underlying HTML document that produces a Web page when viewed with a Web browser. Most Web browsers allow a user to "view" the source document of any page found on the Web.

spam 1. E-mail sent to large numbers of recipients without their first requesting it. 2. Postings of irrelevant messages to newsgroups or listservs. 3. Any attempt to push unwanted information on Internet users by making use of repetitious computing power. 4. (Rarely used) (*cap.*) A pork-based luncheon meat.

subject directory See *search index.*

surfing The process of navigating from site to site on the Internet (usually the Web) in a nonlinear and non-hierarchical manner.

tags (HTML) Commands in HTML documents contained in angled brackets. Tags usually work in pairs, with a closing tag dictating where the effect of the tag ends.

targeting Connecting directly to a Web site or Gopherhost by entering a known address.

Telnet A terminal emulation protocol. With a Telnet client application, such as NCSA Telnet, you can establish a connection to a remote computer.

text only See *ASCII text.*

thread A newsgroup or listserv posting and a series of replies on the same topic, usually with the same subject heading.

tunneling Accessing a site (usually a Gopher site) by digging down through various directories or sub-directories.

Unix See *operating system.* See also *platform.*

uploading Placing a file or application on a remote host over the Internet. Often used to put text, sound, graphics, video, and HTML files on a Web server for publication.

URL (Uniform Resource Locator) The address assigned to each document on the Internet. Consists of the protocol, followed by two slashes, the domain name and type, the directory path, and the file name.

Usenet Part of the Internet which facilitates the exchange of messages and discussion. The broad classification of Usenet contains thousands of topic-centered newsgroups organized hierarchically by name.

Veronica A search engine which can locate items on most of the Internet's Gopher servers using keywords and Boolean operators.

WAIS (Wide Area Information Search) A search engine configured to locate and retrieve information from a designated set of documents. Unlike Veronica or the Web search engines, WAIS performs local rather than general Internet searches.

WAV An audio file format.

Web browser See *browser.*

window A framed area on a computer screen that allows the user to view information without affecting the rest of the screen.

Windows See *operating system.*

workstation An individual computer usually connected to a network but primarily occupied by a single user. Used throughout this book to designate a personal computer where a user can operate local client software.

World Wide Web Abbreviated *WWW* or *the Web.* A worldwide system for distributing hypermedia, allowing users to easily navigate between sites and post their own documents.

For more information about computer terms, visit the Free On-Line Dictionary of Computing at *http://wfn-shop .princeton.edu/cgi-bin/foldoc/.*

Index